# The Waverley Route
## Its Heritage and Revival
### Ann Glen

Lily Publications

**Previous page:** This A3 locomotive, a class long associated with the Waverley route, pounds north up the 1 in 80 slope as it approaches Whitrope with a freight train from Carlisle for Niddrie on 2 December 1961. The engine is BR No. 60068 *Sir Visto* and the dusting of snow reveals a well maintained line. (WS Sellar)

**Lily**
Publications

**About the author**

Ann Glen comes from a family of civil and mechanical engineers with links to railways. She is a graduate of Glasgow and Strathclyde Universities, a Fellow of the Royal Scottish Geographical Society, and by profession a geographer and economic historian. Her career has covered teaching, lecturing and research.

With an interest in transport history, especially relating to railways, she is the co-author of several books, notably on the Caledonian and Great North of Scotland Railways. Other publications have been 'The Cairngorm Gateway' (Scottish Cultural Press, 2003) , the 'Airdrie-Bathgate Rail Link – Reconnecting Communities' (Lily Publications, 2010) and 'Waverley, A Novel Railway Station' (Lily Publications, 2013). She also supports several centres and initiatives for railway heritage. Now active in local government, she serves on a Community Council in North Lanarkshire and represents Strathclyde on the Scottish Association for Public Transport.

# Foreword

## The Right Honourable Lord Steel of Aikwood, KT, KBE, PC

This book could not come at a more appropriate time as we look forward to the re-opening of part of the Waverley Route from Edinburgh to Tweedbank. This fascinating volume tells the story of the construction of railways through the Borders, starting in the first half of the nineteenth century until the error of closure in 1969.

I say 'error' because insufficient attention was paid both by British Rail and by the Department of Transport to the excellent Hibbs Report that recommended retention of the northern portion of the line from Edinburgh to Hawick. This would have been on the basis of de-manning the stations and single-tracking most of the line. The result of that failure is an expensive rail project just to reinstate 30 miles of what was then proposed.

Dr Glen is an acknowledged expert on Scottish railways and knows that all the re-opened lines in Scotland have met or exceeded their passenger traffic estimates. We must hope that the same will be true for the Borders Railway. Subsequently, there may be a case for extending the line the short distance to Hawick.

Meantime, having been a passenger on the last train out of Galashiels in January 1969, I hope to be on board the first one back to the town in 2015. I believe that this book is a worthy tribute to the famous Waverley Route and will add greatly to our enjoyment of the Borders Railway.

*David Steel*

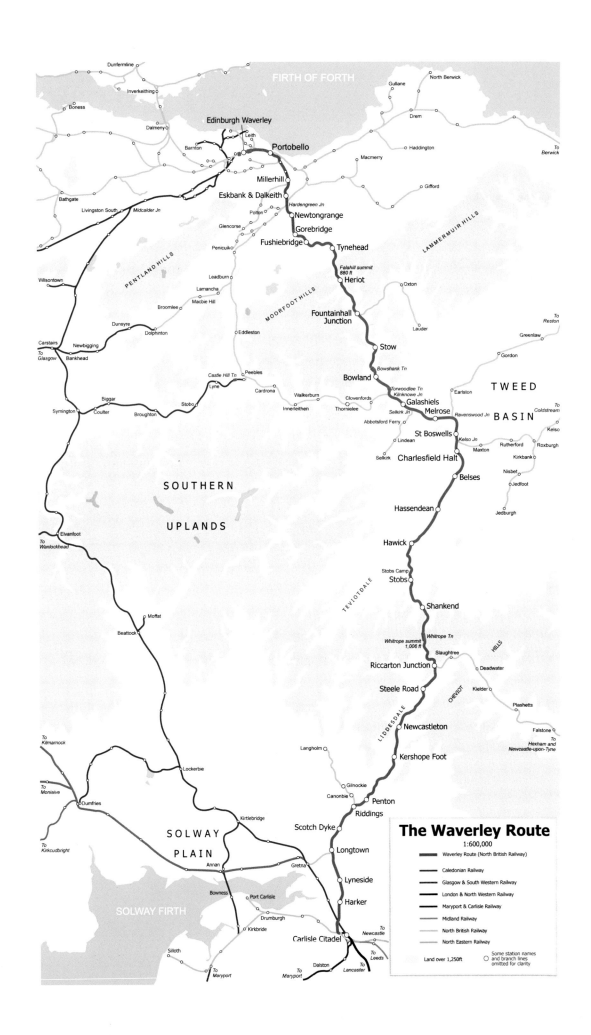

# The Waverley Route

1:600,000

- Waverley Route (North British Railway)
- Caledonian Railway
- Glasgow & South Western Railway
- London & North Western Railway
- Maryport & Carlisle Railway
- Midland Railway
- North British Railway
- North Eastern Railway

Land over 1,250ft    ○ Some station names and branch lines omitted for clarity

FIRTH OF FORTH

Dunfermline
Inverkeithing
Boness
Dalmeny
Barnton
Bathgate
Livingston South
Midcalder Jn
Wilsontown
Carstairs
To Glasgow
Newbigging
Bankhead
Dunsyre
Dolphinton
Symington
Biggar
Coulter
Broughton
Elvanfoot
To Wanlockhead
Moffat
Beattock
To Kilmarnock
Lockerbie
To Moniaive
Dumfries
To Kirkcudbright
Kirtlebridge
Annan
Bowness
Port Carlisle
Drumburgh
Kirkbride
Silloth
To Maryport
Dalston
To Maryport
Gretna
To Newcastle
To Leeds
To Lancaster

Edinburgh Waverley
Leith
Portobello
Millerhill
Eskbank & Dalkeith
Hardengreen Jn
Polton
Newtongrange
Glencorse
Gorebridge
Penicuiko
Fushiebridge
Tynehead
Falahill summit 880 ft
Leadburn
Heriot
Lamancha
Macbie Hill
Broomlee
Fountainhall Junction
Eddleston
Stow
Peebles
Castle Hill Tn
Bowshank Tn
Lyne
Cardrona
Bowland
Stobo
Walkerburn
Torwoodlee Tn
Innerleithen
Thornielee
Clovenfords
Galashiels
Selkirk Jn
Melrose
Abbotsford Ferry
Lindean
St Boswells
Selkirk
Charlesfield Halt
Belses
Hassendean
Hawick
Stobs Camp
Stobs
Shankend
Whitrope summit 1,006 ft
Whitrope Tn
Slaughtree
Riccarton Junction
Steele Road
Newcastleton
Langholm
Kershope Foot
Gilnockie
Canonbie
Penton
Riddings
Scotch Dyke
Longtown
Lyneside
Harker
Carlisle Citadel

PENTLAND HILLS
MOORFOOT HILLS
LAMMERMUIR HILLS
Oxton
Lauder
To Reston
Greenlaw
Gordon
TWEED BASIN
Earlston
Ravenswood Jn
To Coldstream
Kelso
Kelso Jn
Rutherford
Roxburgh
Maxton
Kirkbank
Nisbet
Jedfoot
Jedburgh
Klinknowe Jn

SOUTHERN UPLANDS

TEVIOTDALE

LIDDESDALE

CHEVIOT
HILLS
Deadwater
Kielder
Plashetts
Falstone
To Hexham and Newcastle-upon-Tyne

SOLWAY PLAIN
SOLWAY FIRTH

Macmerry
Haddington
Gifford
To Berwick
Gullane
North Berwick
Drem

# Contents

The Midland and North British Railways aspired to offer luxury
travel for passengers in first class on the Waverley Route –
here with a Dining Carriage in the 1900s. (British Rail)

# Introduction

In the 1960s, the Waverley Route was a topic of conversation – and speculation – in my parents' house for long enough. Would it, or would it not, be axed under the Beeching proposals? Might it be possible to save it in whole, or in part? The twists and turns in the campaigns 'for' and 'against' were followed avidly, and decades on, there are those who continue to regret its closure.

While my family has long-standing railway links, it had only tenuous ones with the Borders, unlike Elizabeth Pryde who has shared her recollections with me. From 1946 her father was Station Master at Heriot, a duty that also covered Falahill, a location notorious for harsh weather and snow blocks. In the severe winter of 1947, trains were trapped there by drifts. For rescuing passengers and carrying many to shelter, her father received a meritorious award from the LNER. Elizabeth was brought up in the Station House, now removed to make way for the Borders Railway. She went to Heriot Primary School and her affinity with the Borders is strengthened further by the fact that she was christened with water from the Gala itself.

When it was announced that the northern 30 miles or so of the Waverley Route was to be revived, this was exciting news for me. Although information had been gathered about the line over the years, a book would be a challenge and there would be much to comprehend. So it was back to 'basics' using the methods applied to record the rebuilding of the Airdrie-Bathgate Rail Link that opened in 2010.

Following geographical practice, there was preliminary desk research, with maps, photographs and documents in archives. This was then interspersed with fieldwork – getting to know the abandoned route by observation and through the soles of the boots. Such investigations began on site – tramping along the 'black paths' installed for cycling and walking where trains had once run, exploring the overgrown track bed in the countryside, or visiting station sites to see buildings that had since found other uses.

A breakthrough came when engineers, equally curious about the line's past, offered a trip over the solum in a 4 x 4 vehicle from one end to the other – in so far as the gaps left by missing bridges and other obstacles would permit. This excursion again revealed just how far nature had reclaimed a double track main line for its own purposes. When the project for the Borders Railway went into construction mode, through the courtesy of Network Rail, the opportunity arose of making many more accompanied visits to sites, especially in the north section. These soon gave an insight into the complexity of the project and the engineering solutions being applied to it.

A travel pass for rail journeys to Newcraighall was invaluable but occasionally bus access was used – a matter of shake, rattle and roll along the A7, a convincing demonstration, if any were required, as to why the railway should be reinstated. In addition, visits were supplemented by assistance from fellow railway enthusiasts eager to keep tabs on the project's progress and to take photographs of it. Altogether over eighty visits, including two phases of residence, were made.

Note had already been taken of potential vantage points, such as over bridges, that would assist photography. Armed with two cameras and a 'step up' to see over raised parapets, a store of images charting progress was gathered. On the whole, the weather throughout the works was remarkably benign with mild, if wet, winters. However, the images tend to show sunny conditions, not so much the result of meteorology and what the Scottish Borders can offer, but of the photographer's choice – only venturing out when conditions were tolerable.

This book is a tribute to engineers, past and present, whose work can be transformational. Engineers should take pride in the fact that their profession can make a greater positive difference to people than almost any other human endeavour.

However, the significance of engineering is seldom sufficiently appreciated by the wider society and economy. Some engineers claim that they 'do not do history', but may be this book will alter that attitude and put their endeavours, not only on record, but also in perspective.

Close to where the Scottish Borders meet Midlothian, a Class 158 DMU passes the summit at Falahill on 8 June 2015. (John Peter)

Thomas Telford, a Borderer born at Langholm, became a
renowned civil engineer and first President of the
Institution of Civil Engineers.

# From Waggonways to Branch Lines

The revival of the northern portion of the Waverley Route – the Borders Railway, so long awaited – has at last become a reality. Over four decades have elapsed since the last passenger trains ran and the new line is very different from the old double track formation.

The first serious proposal for a line through the Borders came in 1809.

*'A MEETING is requested at Fortune's Tavern, Edinburgh, of gentlemen inclined to promote an iron railroad from the Monkland Canal to Lanark, Peebles, Kelso and Berwick-upon-Tweed'*. – The Glasgow Herald, 2 June 1809

As early as 1800, Thomas Telford, the renowned civil engineer, had 'strongly recommended' the use of iron railways as an alternative to canals. He surveyed such a route commencing at Glasgow, a preferred starting point for this 'cast iron railway'. Although Telford was a canal expert, he had used rail systems to facilitate construction on several projects. As was his custom, for the route into the Borders, he walked every mile, taking measurements and making notes. Apart from two short inclined planes operated by stationary steam engines near the headwaters of the Clyde, the system would have been horse-hauled with a gentle gradient of only 1 in 117. Passing through Galashiels, the purpose was to take coal, iron and lime from the west of Scotland to the Borders and bring back foodstuffs, such as grain and livestock produce, for the growing industrial population of the west. The plan for this railroad was never implemented. Later Telford had an advisory role on a number of projects involving steam locomotion, and made useful contributions to the Liverpool & Manchester (1830), to the Newcastle & Carlisle (1834) and other railways.

In the 1820s Robert Stevenson, the famed engineer of Scottish lighthouses, also made surveys with a view to the coming of railways and gave suggestions for likely routes for these. Given the country's landforms, the choices were often restricted, but the valley lying between the Moorfoot and Lammermuir Hills leading to the Gala Water, and thus to the Tweed basin, was identified as having potential for a line. In 1821 his survey for a horse-drawn tramway from Dalkeith to St Boswells attracted the interest of several landed proprietors. Among these was Sir Walter Scott, the eminent author and Laird of Abbotsford, who thus played his part in discussions for early 'iron roads' in the Borders.

The Stevenson route was similar to that of the present Borders Railway with Middleton Moss (north of Falahill) crossed by an iron chain bridge 500yds (457 m) long, and a similar bridge would have spanned the Tweed at Galafoot. After estimating expenses of land purchase and construction, a dividend of 7½ per cent was forecast. Revenue would have been earned from the transport of coal and lime, charged at two pence per ton/mile. Other 'imports' were expected to be timber, iron, oak bark (for tanning), and groceries, but no allowance for 'exports' was made. Although designed for goods and mineral traffic, it was possible that *'were the railway established, there can be little doubt that vehicles might be constructed for the transit of passengers'*. An 'unexplained cause', probably difficulties in raising capital, led to the scheme being abandoned.

Writing in 1824, Charles Maclaren, the far-seeing editor of 'The Scotsman', while acknowledging that railways were 'a recent innovation', stressed the potential of steam locomotives. He believed these would give railways 'a decided superiority' over other forms of land transport and offer 'prospects of almost boundless improvement', an opinion that received widespread publicity both in Europe and America. By 1825, Stephenson locomotives were plying on the Stockton & Darlington Railway, and five years later, the Liverpool & Manchester Railway serving both passengers and freight was opened. In Scotland, the

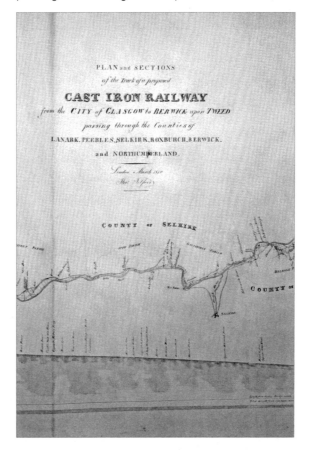

The Galashiels portion of Telford's plan for the 'Glasgow & Berwick Cast Iron Railway' of 1809 showing this section's gentle gradient profile.

(Glen Collection)

**Above:** Sir Walter Scott, the laird of Abbotsford and historical novelist, was an early supporter of railways in the Borders. (National Portrait Gallery of Scotland)

**Above right:** Waggonways with horse haulage were the forerunners of the railways wherever minerals had to be transported. (British Library)

Garnkirk & Glasgow of 1831 was another triumph for Robert Stephenson and his engines.

Promotional meetings soon took place about an Anglo-Scottish route on the east coast, and the name 'The Great North British Railway' appeared. A line was surveyed to come north from Hexham on the Newcastle & Carlisle Railway that had opened in 1839. This would have connected Melrose and Galashiels with Edinburgh but a 3 mile long tunnel (4.8 km) under the Cheviot Hills was enough to rule it out.

As yet there was no firm proposal for a rail link between Scotland and England. In 1841 promoters of a 'National Railway of Scotland', with its focus centred on Peebles, foresaw tracks coming to that burgh from Lancaster via Carlisle. The line would then divide connecting with Glasgow and Edinburgh. A Royal Commission took the view that a single Anglo-Scottish route would suffice, and this would be a West Coast route from London via Crewe to Carlisle; from there it would go by Annandale over Beattock Summit dividing at Carstairs to serve Glasgow and Edinburgh. This was subsequently completed by the Caledonian Railway in 1848.

By 1842, the Edinburgh & Glasgow Railway, Scotland's first main line, was in action. Locomotives were running on it at 30mph or more and the E&G was a huge success. Its chairman was John Learmonth, a wealthy Edinburgh man and former Lord Provost (1831) who purchased the Dean estate. With an interest in transport through his family's coach building business, he had Telford design the imposing Dean Bridge over the Water of Leith. Learmonth was determined to see the railway reach the centre of Edinburgh – as it did on 22 June 1846 to the site where Waverley station stands today. But he had another ambition – to develop an Edinburgh & Berwick Railway, ultimately established as part of an East Coast route and owned by a North British Railway Company. Only lack of money stood in the way and English investors became a likely source of capital.

When an Act was sought for the NBR's proposed line to Berwick-on-Tweed in 1844, it attracted strenuous opposition from the Edinburgh & Dalkeith Railway, a waggonway system in the Lothians on the 4ft 6in 'Scotch gauge'. This had branches carrying coal for export to harbours on the Forth shores at Fisherrow and at Leith that would be cut through by the NBR's proposed East Coast route.

As long ago as 1826, the E&DR had been approved by an Act of Parliament. Its engineer was James Jardine, Dumfries-shire born and a graduate of Edinburgh University.

A surviving warehouse at the former St Leonards depot of the Edinburgh & Dalkeith Railway from where coal was distributed to the city.

At a time when roads were poor and often impassable, the line's purpose was to supply Lothian coal to the city's households and industries, and to meet this objective, a depot was set up at St Leonards below Salisbury Crags. A feature of the E&DR at that point was a long tunnel – the first on any Scottish line – with a steep slope worked as an inclined plane by stationary steam engines and lit by gas.

There was a long history of coal working in the Lothians. From the Middle Ages, the monks of Newbattle Abbey had used coal to heat salt pans, fire kilns and warm monastic quarters. They had interests as far away as present day Lanarkshire – hence its old name of 'Monklands'. After the Reformation in 1560 and the dissolution of the monasteries, regal favourites and power brokers emerged as big landowners. By the eighteenth century, coal workings were growing and the 'coal barons' – wealthy and influential men, including the Duke of Buccleuch, the Earl of Dalhousie and the Marquis of Lothian – were leasing pits to coal masters to exploit.

Initially the coal seams could be accessed off the riversides where the North and South Esk and their tributaries had cut ravine-like valleys. The geology was to prove complex with the seams commonly faulted and fractured, many being 'on end' at the margin of the Esk coal basin. Simple 'in-gaun' ee' (in-going eye) or tunnel mines were later supplemented by bell pits excavated from the surface. However, water readily drained into these and the sides were prone to collapse. Once stationary steam engines were available, water could be pumped out and coal lifted from greater depths. The place name 'Arniston Engine' recalls such an installation. . The working of seams by the 'stoop and room' method came to the fore, where the 'stoops' were pillars of coal left to hold up the roof. Over time these decayed and subsided, leaving hummocky and unstable ground.

The E&DR was mainly double tracked and horse-hauled throughout its existence. Opened to the nearest coal pit on 4 July 1831, it grew to be a network of some 12 miles continuing east by Duddingston Loch, Niddrie, Millerhill and Hardengreen to Dalhousie (Newtongrange). To cross the deep valley of the North Esk, Jardine designed a magnificent masonry bridge with single track at Glenesk; dating from 1831, this semi-circular arch is the oldest on any Scottish line. From its north side, a short branch to Dalkeith was subsequently built and opened in 1838. As the Duke of Buccleuch owned coal pits at Cowden and Smeaton near that town, he had an extension made at his own expense in 1839 to serve these for which a large viaduct with masonry piers and timber arches had to be constructed over the North Esk.

Further south came the Dalhousie viaduct across the South Esk. Over 1,000ft long, this pioneering structure had 24 spans of cast iron and timber. The design was by John Williamson, a colliery manager on the Dalhousie estate. An advertisement invited *'Founders, Builders, Contractors and Wood Merchants for Furnishing a considerable quantity of Cast Iron Beams and Cast Iron Arches for Railway Bridges, and other materials, notably Timber Beams...'* The Scotsman 20 March 1830

At Dalhousie, the E&DR met the Marquis of Lothian's Waggonway close to an alignment that the revived Borders Railway follows.

Although the Edinburgh & Dalkeith Railway conveyed about 300 tons of coal per day to the city, it also offered passenger trips using converted stagecoaches. These gave

Edinburgh folk a taste for rail travel of an informal kind, and soon 300,000 or more a year were sampling jaunts into the countryside. In 1833 there were seven coaches a day each way between Edinburgh and Gorebridge, the line giving passengers the option of seeing local attractions or taking a short walk to Fushiebridge with its good inn. There were no intermediate stations or tickets, passengers boarding or alighting where they chose on what became known as 'The Innocent Railway'. Latterly, half the E&DR receipts came from passengers and such a journey through the countryside was later recalled:

*'The rich flat valley through which we rolled ...veined with rail-ways branching off, right and left, to the several coal-works – to Edmonstone, Newton, Sir John's, &c, &c'.*

– John Johnstone 4 August 1832

At that time there was an embargo on the use of steam locomotives on the E&DR but its rural charm was soon to be disturbed.

Railway development in Britain came to the fore in the mid-1840s when it was realised just how convenient and profitable lines could be. Railways were rapidly expanding economic activity, and indeed were becoming major

Landowners, such as the Dukes of Buccleuch, had a profound influence on railway development. The grounds of Dalkeith Palace, bordering the Edinburgh & Hawick Railway, are now a Country Park while the mansion is leased to the Universlity of Wisconsin. (Glen Collection)

The Glenesk viaduct, an impressive structure on the Edinburgh & Dalkeith Railway, designed by James Jardine and dating from 1831, spans the gorge of the North Esk. (Martin Powers, Network Rail)

The first Dalhousie viaduct on the Marquis of Lothian's Waggonway was also built in 1831 and used timber, cast iron and some masonry piers. (National Library of Scotland Map Room)

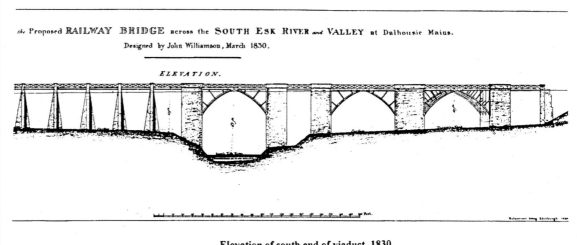

*the* Proposed RAILWAY BRIDGE across the SOUTH ESK RIVER *and* VALLEY at Dalhousie Mains.

Designed by John Williamson, March 1830.

*ELEVATION.*

**Elevation of south end of viaduct 1830.**

industries in their own right. Lines could have a phenomenal impact on both economy and society through their speed of communication – as the rails advanced, distances simply shrank. However, a 'free-for-all' of rail development had to be restrained and in 1844 a Railway Act was passed when William Gladstone, a politician of Scottish descent, was President of the Board of Trade. It attached certain conditions to the construction of future railways. Under this new law, all carriages had to be covered – with roofs to give protection – and they must also have seats. To restrain overcharging, railway companies had to provide on each of their lines 'conveyance for Third Class passengers', at the cost of one penny a mile, at least once a day in each direction – the so-called 'Parliamentary trains'. Their average speed was to be not less than 12 miles per hour (19km/h). The Act also threatened a state takeover of railways if the private companies failed to cooperate.

From the profits arising from factories and mills, new middle class money was increasingly available for investment, and government bonds, once considered 'safe' appeared much less rewarding than railway stock. This was yielding 5 per cent or more. Investors, especially in Lancashire, were enthusiasts for railway companies and 'Railway Mania' took off. There was intense competition to lay claim to both capital and territory, leading to the promotion of numerous lines for which Bills had to be drawn up and Acts of Parliament obtained.

Old stagecoaches were adapted for passenger use on the Edinburgh & Dalkeith Railway, thereby giving people a taste for rail travel. (Durham Advertiser)

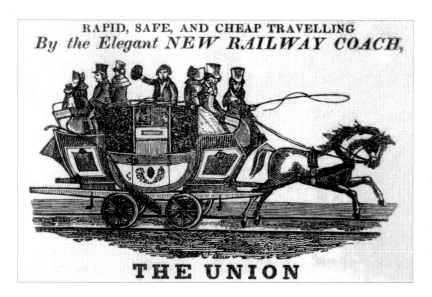

**RAPID, SAFE, AND CHEAP TRAVELLING**
*By the Elegant NEW RAILWAY COACH,*

**THE UNION**

Proposals for trunk lines came to typify the boom years and the name of George Hudson, a Yorkshire entrepreneur, came to the fore. By amalgamations and takeovers, this 'Railway King' soon controlled over 1,000 miles of tracks reaching out from York throughout the Midlands. In 1844 he was the founding father of the York & North Midland Railway that eventually became the Midland Railway Company, but he was also the mastermind for an East Coast route from England to Scotland. When the NBR asked for financial advice, Hudson suggested that Lancashire money might be utilised and he himself cast eyes on the proposed Scottish enterprise.

The North British Railway Company therefore tapped into Lancashire money and its very name may have been chosen to give reassurance – after all, it was only one hundred years since a Jacobite rebellion, when an invasion of England as far as Derby, had taken place. John Learmonth, now chairman of the NBR, worked tirelessly to win support for the project and to drive forward the East Coast route from Edinburgh.

When the speculation was at its height in 1844-45, plans for thousands of miles of railway were deposited, with some consulting engineers specialising in promoting or opposing Railway Bills. There were many Scottish schemes – 110 were listed in 1845 alone – each with a prospectus indicating possible returns in glowing terms. Investors pored over newspaper reports and read such journals as the *Scottish Railway Gazette* to follow trends in stocks and shares being traded at silly prices.

A springboard for any advance into the Borders was the Edinburgh & Dalkeith Railway and that company initially promoted its own Edinburgh & Hawick Railway Bill. As it resolutely opposed the North British Company's proposal for an East Coast main line, the E&DR even threatened to make a line of its own to join either the Caledonian route coming north to Carstairs, or the Edinburgh & Glasgow Railway. However, the North British directors simply could not allow the E&DR to play into the hands of potential rivals – and they were also determined to keep other railway companies out of the Lothians. The outcome was an offer to purchase the E&DR for £113,000, a settlement considered generous at the time, and it was accepted. During its existence, that early railway had contributed much 'to the commerce, convenience and health of the surrounding neighbourhood'. On 4 July 1844, an Act was obtained for

the North British route from Edinburgh to Berwick-on-Tweed.

The Board of Trade had reflected again upon Anglo-Scottish lines, continuing to favour the Caledonian Railway's Annandale route over Beattock Summit. Meanwhile, the NBR was proposing a branch of its own from Edinburgh to Hawick. The subscribers to its Edinburgh & Hawick Railway show great diversity – from the Lord Chief Justice, aristocrats, assorted reverends, army officers, surgeons, bankers and land owners to mill owners and merchants of every sort, all individuals with money to invest in the new mode of transport. John Learmonth himself was an investor in several Scottish companies. About 10 per cent of the investors were women – some titled and wealthy, others of modest means.

Controversially, a pledge was offered to take the line to Carlisle, thereby 'giving a communication from Edinburgh to the West of England (i.e. Lancashire) and the manufacturing districts' of its influential investors. The Board of Trade was unimpressed, viewing it as 'absolutely inconsistent to have a trunk line from Edinburgh to Carlisle by way of Hawick'.

The Board was also cautious about the prospects for the NBR's Edinburgh & Hawick Railway, advising that it would only be for 'local accommodation', while giving a better connection to Edinburgh. Most of all, by lowering the price of coal, it would be advantageous for the thriving woollen industries of Galashiels and Hawick. At the time, coal was being carted in 1½ ton loads to the mills, 'at heavy expense from the vicinity of Dalkeith'. The report's chairman and vice-president of the Board of Trade was the 9th Earl of Dalhousie, who certainly had an interest in the

railway being built – he was a major coal owner. However, there were still doubts about the line's viability and potential return on capital:

*'If constructed cheaply, the traffic might be sufficient to afford a modest remuneration to the North British Company …whose Dalkeith line will be a feeder'.*
– Parliamentary Papers XXXIX (120) 1845

For the NBR, the old 'Dalkeith line' was in fact a bonus giving it not only a coal depot at St Leonards in Edinburgh, but also a marketing organisation for the effective distribution of fuel in the city.

As regards building the new railway cheaply, the NBR became well versed in making money stretch, but would traffic ever justify the capital to be invested in the Edinburgh & Hawick Railway? (The estimate of expense was put at £400,000, the capital or stock at £460,000 and the money authorised to be borrowed at £133,333. Initially, only £32,000 in £1 shares had been subscribed). By 1846 the speculative bubble of the 'Railway Mania' burst and share prices collapsed just when the E&HR had scarcely been begun. The frenzy for railway shares made some people very rich, but without limited liability, it ruined many others. Enthusiasm for new lines therefore cooled. By 1848 Hudson had been dealt another blow by trade depression and forced into bankruptcy. Nevertheless, from the mid-1840s onwards, an immense and useful mileage of railways was constructed, and within a decade most of the main lines in Britain had been built.

When the Bill for the Edinburgh & Hawick Railway came to be considered by a Parliamentary Committee in May 1845, those in favour or against had to attend the

The view from the Lothianbridge viaduct, formerly known as Dalhousie, showing the A7 road and the Sun Inn behind which the Marquis of Lothian's Waggonway ran.

An excerpt from the plan for the Edinburgh, Hawick & Carlisle Railway of 1844 showing its proposed route through Langholm.
(Buccleuch Archives, Drumlanrig Castle)

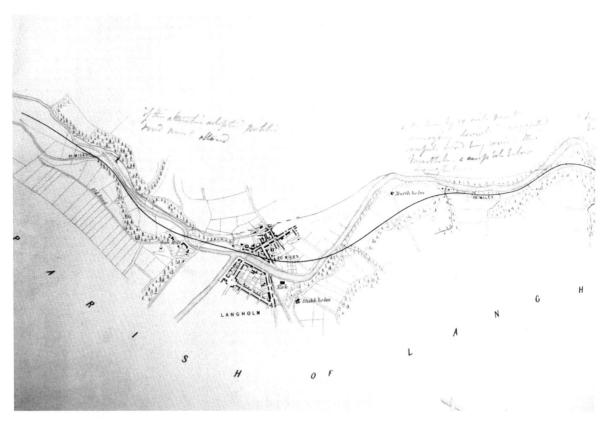

committee hearings at Westminster and defend their positions. A journey to London from Edinburgh took at least two days on a stagecoach as the East Coast main line had yet to be completed. It was a tiresome and expensive trip that only the determined, and those who were obliged to do so, would make.

The 'Opposed Bills' reveal what varied interests the E&HR witnesses had – there were land and property owners, woollen manufacturers, colliery lessees, lawyers and a surprising number of civil engineers. Foremost among these was Isambard Kingdom Brunel, who appeared twice before a Select Committee of the House of Lords on behalf of the E&HR. He was already a celebrity on account of the Great Western Railway, completed on the broad gauge of 7ft from Paddington to Bristol Temple Meads in 1841, and required no introduction. It was a time of debate about

Stone sleepers from an early waggonway, the Monkland & Kirkintilloch Railway, on display at the Summerlee Heritage Centre at Coatbridge. A horse could plod along the line between such sleepers.

suitable track width for a national network, the so-called 'Battle of the Gauges'. (This led to Parliament appointing a Gauge Commission that reported in 1846 in favour of the standard gauge of 4ft 8½in. This was an acute disappointment for Brunel. The broad gauge became a feature solely on the Great Western Railway where its supporters believed it would allow the attainment of 'a high rate of speed' and thus produce 'a maximum profit').

Regarding the proposals for the E&HR, Brunel was questioned by men who knew very little about railways or engineering, but with Parliament having to consider so many Bills they were having to learn fast. The famous engineer required no introduction:

*Q. Will you look at the plans for this railway. Do you see any gradients or find any curve that should prohibit the construction of this line?*

*IKB. There is a gradient here on 1 in 75 with sharp curves 20 chains radius – if the country requires these gradients and curves – of which I cannot judge (I do not know the country)...they could be worked.*

*Q. There is no doubt about that? IKB. No. Q. Worked with safety? IKB. Yes.*

To have an eminent engineer such as Brunel take part in the proceedings was a masterstroke, and to hear him make such statements about the railway's proposed alignment must have been encouraging for the promoters of the E&HR. There were, of course, no such curves or gradients on his Great Western Railway from Paddington to Bristol where the steepest section was Box Tunnel at 1 in 100.

But to return to the Borders:

*Q. "Have you been over this line?" IKB. "No".*

*Q. "You are unable to say whether the country itself will admit of better gradients and less severe curves being taken?" IKB. "I cannot".*

*Q. "Do you mean it is a practical line for both passenger and goods traffic?"*

*IKB. "I mean for both".*

Brunel never visited Scotland. Would there be 'any apprehension of danger' for the public in travelling on such a curving and steep line? "Certainly not" was his response. As an example, he cited the tight curve on the Bristol & Exeter line near Bristol station that trains 'always traversed at high speed'.

*Q. Your reputation is that you avoid bad curves as much as you can?*

*IKB. So does every engineer. We run at high speed at 1 in 80 – and if there is no danger in that, there can hardly be danger in 1 in 75'.*

Generally, trains on the Great Western Railway were capable of 30 to 35 mph, a sensation in the 1840s.

With the proposed E&HR on a long embankment – the famous Borthwick Bank – he foresaw no difficulty on that account either. When asked about the safety of descents on curving lines, he suggested a 'brake carriage' on the tail of a train to supplement what braking was possible with a locomotive and tender. (He pointed out that this was a solution used successfully on the 1 in 37 Lickey Incline south of Birmingham).

Brunel was questioned again about the long steep incline of 8 miles south from Dalhousie and the many sharp curves on the route. Referring to the Great Western Railway's line, under construction to Cornwall, he disclosed that he was currently *'making works …in Devonshire with 1 in 40 gradients and curves of 20 chains'*.

When Brunel was asked if a speed restriction of 10 to 15mph – on trains going down the incline north from Falahill – would reduce risks, he believed it would:

*Q. Do you think the regulation could be enforced? You think it very difficult?*

*IKB. Yes … I do not think either the locomotive men or the parties working the line would feel there was any danger'.*

He therefore doubted the speed limit's effectiveness in practice. As the E&HR was proposed as a single track, would it be liable to the risk of collisions? His answer was 'yes' and that he was 'adverse' to single lines on all occasions. Nevertheless, the electric telegraph 'would diminish the danger very much'. For his evidence as an expert witness, Brunel was paid a fee of £52.10s, (the equivalent of a stationmaster's salary for a year at that date). Some engineers specialised in supporting or opposing Railway Bills, such interventions providing a useful stream of extra income.

Another key witness was John Miller (1803-1883) of the Edinburgh & Glasgow Railway who would be the engineer for the new branch. Ayrshire born, he had forsaken law for mathematics and trained in land surveying. In 1825 he became the partner of Thomas Grainger in Edinburgh and in 1832 achieved membership of the Institution of Civil Engineers. He gained much experience on the Edinburgh & Glasgow Railway, opened in 1842, for which Grainger & Miller were the engineers. For the E&HR, Miller was asked to produce 'a good working line at a cost which will show a handsome return'. Improvements in the 'locomotive engine' were by then reducing the extent of cuttings, embankments and viaducts – railways need no longer be as level and straight as possible, and consequently became less expensive to make. Lines steeper than 1 in 200 were now thought 'unobjectionable', while slopes of 1 in 50 to 1 in 100 were considered 'perfectly practicable'. Making sharper curves also had the effect of reducing construction costs.

Unlike Brunel, Miller was unknown in the south of England and thus had to be introduced to the House of Lords Committee:

*'Q. You are a Civil Engineer? JM. Yes. Q. You have already constructed I believe several Railways in Scotland? JM. Yes. Q. In fact, there is hardly a railway in Scotland but what you are connected with? JM. Most of them, I believe'.*

The partnership of Grainger & Miller deposited plans for over 1,500 miles of railway in the 1840s.

Asked to point out the course of the line to 'their Lordships', Miller indicated Dalhousie Mains and the existing waggonway, 'originally only a mineral line'.

He was well informed not only about other Scottish proposals, many of which he had indeed surveyed, but also

The renowned engineer Isambard Kingdom Brunel spoke in favour of the Edinburgh & Hawick Railway at the Bill Committee at the House of Lords in 1845.

(Wikipedia)

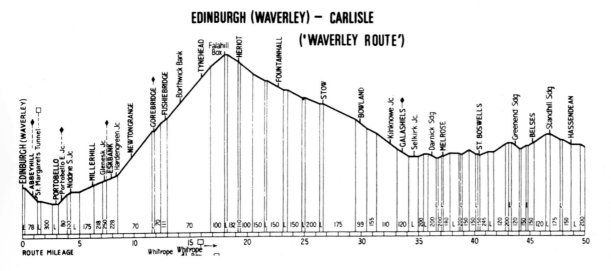

The gradient profile of the Edinburgh & Hawick Railway showing the testing ascents going south from Hardengreen to Falahill and from Galashiels northwards.

(BR Scottish Region)

A portrait of John Miller CE, FRSE, the engineer for the Edinburgh & Hawick Railway, shows him wearing his spectacles. (National Portrait Gallery of Scotland)

about English ones. Knowing the lie of the land in the Borders, he acknowledged the limited choice of route through the Southern Uplands to take a railway to the Gala Water and the River Tweed.

Miller and the NBR were also far seeing – although the E&HR might be constructed as a single line, the bridges and other structures would be built with a view to doubling in the interests of safety. To save money, Miller preferred cuttings to tunnels and was also satisfied with gradients of 1 in 75 and curves of 20 chains radius. He also noted that the power of locomotives had increased greatly and that the Caledonian Railway (then proposed coming north over Beattock summit) had long stretches at 1 in 75 to 1 in 80 that the Board of Trade found acceptable. But could lesser gradients be obtained 'at an expense which the traffic of the country could bear'?

*JM. No… It is hilly country – either have a line such as this, or be without one altogether. The midland ridge forms an obstacle obstructing a railway in that country… It would require an enormous amount to improve the gradients to any extent… the broad ridge cannot be easily cut through.'*

The 'midland ridge' to which he was referring was the Southern Uplands.

Even so, there would be one tunnel on the line, 'nearly on the summit' with a gradient of 1 in 75. This was at Tynehead where bores had been taken in clay.

'*Q. You have stated that there is no curve in the tunnel. I think you will find that is wrong'. JM. The tunnel is perfectly straight, that is to say, you can see through it from one end to the other'.*

Nevertheless, the Tynehead tunnel proposal was abandoned, and in order to avoid tight curves on the valley floor at Bowshank 11 miles to the south, a 249yd (227.7m) tunnel was subsequently made there.

Wherever possible, requests for tunnels were resisted. The owner of the Langlee estate east of Galashiels was dissatisfied with the line's 'mode of passing his property'. He had suggested a tunnel but Miller argued that 'the levels would not admit of it'. He also denied there would be serious damage to amenity or residence as the line was 'too far removed' from the house, and, in addition, the line would be hidden in a cutting 39 ft deep (now bridged at Winston Road).

Continuing concerns for the Parliamentary Committee were the curves on the difficult 8 miles up to Falahill, Miller stated there were ten curves:

'*Q. How many of these are a quarter of a mile radius, that is 20 chains radius?*

*JM. Four of them. Q. Is it not six? JM. Six curves? Q. Of 20 chains radius?*

*JM. No, I think not'.*

Some would be on Borthwick Bank, an earthwork 130ft high in places, but Miller saw no cause for alarm as it was 'just about the same as crossing the Tyne at Newcastle'.

However, there would be many more curves along the Gala Water to take the railway south to the River Tweed.

'*Q. You have reason to cross the Gala Water? JM. It is crossed by bridges …by adopting the several river crossings*

*required, it is the cheapest and best mode of going down the valley… it avoids coming in contact with the jutting points that are existing there…'*

Altogether, about 80 bridges 'of one sort and another, great and small, some of them very small' would be necessary. Their total cost would be £32,000, including a new Dalhousie (Lothianbridge) viaduct at £6,000. The under bridges would be of timber, some being on masonry piers, the over bridges of masonry and brick. Miller described the sandstone viaduct crossing the Tweed near Melrose as 'a mere bridge'; it cost £2,000 and is now known as the 'Red Bridge'.

As 'conversations' had been held with the Road Trustees, there was no opposition to level crossings as no main road would be involved at such points. Bridges carrying roads over the railway were acceptable as long as the slopes up and down were not excessively steep for horse traffic. Andrew Pringle, a local farmer at Bowland, appeared as a witness to argue for a low bridge there in preference to a level crossing to protect children going to school at Caitha. They '*deserved a footway under the railway …with a 7ft high arch …to prevent the danger of scholars getting upon the railroad'.* Miller was recalled to explain how this could be done – by building up the embankments at each side, but at more expense. (This exceptionally low bridge, replaced with an iron version in 1884, was only removed in 2013).

Parliamentary Committees were really apprehensive about the descent of slopes on account of the primitive state of brakes on locomotives and tenders. In April 1844 as the 'Railway Mania' took off, a Bill for the Inverness & Perth Railway Company was rejected as there was doubt about the ability of locomotives to take trains 'safely down' the gradients in such mountainous terrain. The Lickey Incline at 1 in 37 was the steepest negotiated to date. Miller was asked about the likely risks on the E&HR:

'*The danger to the public, if there is any, is the descent, but there is no danger as the speed can be regulated to the nicest degree'.*

He then explained that in addition to the brakes, if necessary, steam could be made to work 'the reverse way' in order to bring the train 'perfectly to a standstill' – he did not mention the effect that this extreme action might have on the locomotive.

Altogether, Miller considered the E&HR was 'a very easy line as projected' and would make 'communication possible with the East Coast'. The fact that it was likely to be a single line led to a speed restriction of 15mph being written into the Act as Parliament feared collisions on these. This limit would be a weakness for a passenger railway when relatively fast journeys were becoming the norm. However, the NBR directors were already considering a double track and Miller had estimated for suitable bridges for this enlargement. He put the total outlay for the construction of the E&HR, including land acquisition, at £400,000 with 10 per cent allowed for contingencies. He mentioned 'respectable contractors' for a line that 'could be contracted for tomorrow' at the price of £360,000. But would they be 'solvent persons'? 'Perfectly so' was Miller's positive response, but only time would tell. The NBR's working expenses for the line were estimated at £33,000 – a sum of 40 per cent that he considered 'more than necessary'. Prudently, he had not calculated the likely dividend on capital.

Miller pointed out that the railway would go close to Galashiels, that Selkirk was only 5 miles away and that both

The original low bridge at Bowland, with its 7ft clearance, was built to keep scholars attending the local school off the railway. The timber structure was replaced with iron in the 1880s.

Abbotsford and Melrose were nearby. These places had a special significance – their links with Sir Walter Scott, the acclaimed author of books and poems with historic themes, many of them based in the Borders. Through the 'romantic appeal' of his writings, Walter Scott is credited with 'kick starting' tourism in Scotland. In 1844 the Scott Monument, a noble memorial, was nearing completion in Edinburgh's Princes Street Gardens. Abbotsford would become a literary shrine and over decades the North British Railway would play a key role in bringing tourists to the Scott country.

A representative from the Caledonian Railway's extension line, 'not yet complete' northwards from Carlisle, appeared before the House of Lords Committee. This young engineer had been 'engaged in the construction of the Great Western Railway' as an assistant to Brunel. Although the jibe 'as glib as could be' was levelled at him, he at least knew that timber bridges were not durable when exposed to rivers and adverse weather.

By the 1840s Galashiels was developing as a mill town beside the Gala Water. The name 'shiels' came from the bothies or shelters used by shepherds tending their flocks on the surrounding hills. The woollen industry began in people's cottages where spinning, weaving and knitting of local wool provided essential clothing in a cold climate. From the 1790s the activity had increasingly become mill based, relying on the flow of the Gala Water both for power and processing. George Roberts, a cloth manufacturer with businesses in both Galashiels and Selkirk, was asked about the likely effects of the railway on his trade in tweeds and tartans, 'the finer fabrics of Saxony and other fine wools'. As early as the 1830s, quality wool was being imported from Australia, then known as Van Diemen's Land, and within a decade, 500 tons a year, valued at £100,000, were being used. A mill in Galashiels had even been re-named 'Botany' after the infamous bay. From the 1830s, production had soared but all the valuable waterpower, using weirs or 'cauls'

on the river to feed mill lades, had now been exploited. Demand for woollen goods was outstripping local output and both Galashiels and Selkirk were prospering. Hawick, specialising in hosiery, was also relying on wool imports.

As Roberts explained:

*'We try steam but many people doubt if it will pay – if coal was cheaper, it would be valuable to a greater extent'.*

Even so there were already 30 sets of engines in the mills driving 18,000 spindles to produce yarn. More mills were planned but it was expensive and slow to bring fuel supplies from the Lothian pits in carts along the turnpike road. Not only wool imports but also groceries, were trundled slowly south from Edinburgh. With a 'rail road' constructed, 'the whole of the raw materials' plus many other items could be

The viaduct over the River Tweed east of Galashiels was a 'mere bridge' according to its designer, the engineer John Miller. It is now known as the Red Bridge.

A view of the straggling village of Galashiels, seen from the west, prior to the arrival of the railway.
(Robert Hall, History of Galashiels)

carried, and the savings on coal alone were estimated at 25 per cent a ton. One far-seeing manufacturer in Galashiels had already leased Arniston Colliery near Newtongrange to supply his business with coal.

There was an equally positive response from a Hawick manufacturer as costs for coal and essential supplies – oils, soap, and alkalis – were even higher in that town. For the manufacturers, the railway could not come too soon. The mill owners would benefit, the farmers and the agriculture of the district would gain, as would the local communities accessing more and cheaper supplies, including foodstuffs.

Statistics had been gathered about coach and goods traffic on the turnpike roads. Stagecoaches took some 12,900 passengers from Edinburgh mainly to Melrose, probably attracted by Sir Walter Scott's writings about that locality. Galashiels, Hawick and Selkirk saw just short of 10,000 and Carlisle 6,000 a year. Most goods went to Galashiels and Hawick in carts lumbering along at 3 miles an hour – it was hoped a rail journey would be at least twice as fast.

Negotiating the Act for its 'most ambitious branch' cost the NBR £12,695 and its efforts were successful. On 21 July 1845 the 'North British Railway (Edinburgh & Dalkeith Purchase) Act' conferred the powers for the Edinburgh & Hawick Railway on the NBR. Events moved quickly and on 31 July an Act followed for the NBR's own Edinburgh & Hawick Railway Company. This allowed it to construct a spur from its mainline near Portobello (soon re-named 'Hawick Junction') to the E&DR system at Niddrie – making it possible for trains to run from the NBR's North Bridge station (later Waverley) to Dalhousie and the proposed line to Hawick. The Bill had also sought an extension of the Hawick line to Carlisle, a route that was reported as surveyed, but the scheme was shelved as the Board of Trade did not approve of it. To complete that line as the Waverley Route would become a longstanding ambition for the NBR.

The Act stated that the Edinburgh & Hawick Railway would be constructed 'of such a Width as to admit of laying down thereon a double Line of Rails'. If after a year, 'an additional Line of Rails is required for the Safety and Convenience of the Public' then 'the Lords of the Council for Trade and Plantations' – the Board of Trade – could instruct that this be done. To ensure safe operation, 'a proper Electrical Telegraph along the whole Length of the said Railway for the Transmission of Intelligence' was to be installed. During the 1840s, the first telegraph lines in Britain were appearing on the expanding rail network. These allowed messages in Morse code to be sent between stations along wires held aloft by wooden poles placed beside the track. The Edinburgh & Hawick Railway, like the E&G before it, would have such a system. On the NBR, fixed boards and flags were the basic 'signalising equipment'. A white board indicated a clear road, green was caution and red was stop. By night lamps were lit, a white light showing a clear line ahead and a red lamp, danger.

Some other requirements were also written into the Act; Stobs gunpowder mills at Gorebridge, dating from 1794, had special attention. Powered by ten water wheels, this establishment was the largest of its kind in Scotland. Some 50 to 60 men were employed and the gunpowder was exported 'to every quarter of the globe'. The 'black powder' produced was highly dangerous to manufacture, store and transport, and railway construction used plenty of it – any tunnelling taking a ton a week. For safety reasons, the Act restricted the proximity of the railway to the mills – there was extensive fencing and two short tunnels (now long removed) south of Gorebridge.

A crucial aspect of the Act was the right to purchase land but this could only be exercised for three years – and not more than 50 acres could be taken from any one proprietor. The plans, sections and books of reference, deposited with the Sheriff-Clerks of the counties of Edinburgh, Roxburgh and Selkirk, were available for inspection on payment of one shilling (10p).

The Act specified the fares on the E&HR – 3d per mile for First-class, 2d for Second and 1½d for Third. Passengers were permitted to take some luggage free. If the wealthy

Gorebridge was noted for its gunpowder mills and coal pits, as shown on the First Edition 6 Inch Ordnance Survey map of 1852-3. Note the short tunnels on the railway. (National Library of Scotland Map Room)

so desired, they could travel in their own vehicles placed on a truck at 7d per mile. Charges for freight were detailed – dung and compost at 2d per ton per mile; coal, bricks, clay, iron and the like at 2½d; sugar, grain, nails, and timber at 3d, but manufactured goods, including cotton and wools were 4d per ton. Similarly, the charges for livestock were sheep and small animals at ½d each, cattle at 2d and 'horses, mules and asses' at 5d per mile. Stations would become busy places with both passenger and goods traffic bringing new employment opportunities in the Borders countryside.

With the sale of the E&DR completed by October 1845, what did the NBR get? Basically a waggonway with fish-bellied iron rails on freestone blocks and a very useful coal depot at St Leonards. The conversion from the 'Scotch gauge' to standard gauge was soon in progress with the line also being strengthened to take steam locomotives – the NBR having renounced the E&DR embargo on their use. It was the commencement of a route to the Borders that would present problems down the years not just with its multiple bridges, but also with its curves and awkward hills to ascend and descend. For these reasons, the Board of Trade only saw the Edinburgh & Hawick Railway as a secondary route.

Nevertheless, the directors of the E&HR were men of influence who could talk up the potential of the new line. Together with Learmonth, fellow directors were John Christison and George Turnbull of the Edinburgh & Glasgow Railway, Sir James Forrest was Lord Provost of Edinburgh

and Eagle Henderson was the founder of the Standard Life Insurance Company. In their view the railway 'would be of great public advantage by opening an additional, certain and expeditious Means of Communication' between Edinburgh and Hawick, while 'facilitating contact' with other locations at a distance.

Travel before the railway came to the Borders was a tedious affair. Even in the 1840s solitary travellers on horseback risked being attacked and robbed. Joining a group on a coach gave a safer, if uncomfortable, journey. A contemporary account described the experience:

*'At 4 o'clock the stage coach set off from Edinburgh for Galashiels, 32 miles away, with a dozen passengers booked on board. Once into the countryside, the turnpike road was rough despite signs of recent repairs. After 15 miles there was a brief stop at an inn to allow the three horses to be changed. By now, extra passengers had squeezed on board with some perched perilously on the back. Then on the climb to Falahill, the coach slowed to walking pace. It was after 10 o'clock and dark when it at last*

John Learmonth, first chairman of the North British Railway Company, who believed in the 'great public advantage' that the Edinburgh & Hawick Railway would bring. (Watercolour in St George's Parish Church, Edinburgh)

*rolled into Galashiels, setting the weary passengers down at the Bridge Inn. It had been a six hour journey. How they longed for the railway – it would be so convenient in spite of its smoke, steam and noise – and so much cheaper and faster than travel on any coach'.*

Such passengers would soon see the first trains consisting of four-wheeled carriages, hauled by primitive steam locomotives, clattering along the tracks, conveying people faster than they had ever travelled before. With the Act secured, the Border country was about to have its first railway.

With the Royal Assent given on 31 July 1845, moves for the construction of the North British Company's E&HR could begin. Typically, the Borders and the Lothians were the territory of influential landowners – top of the list was the Duke of Buccleuch, followed by Marquises, Earls and Baronets with large estates where tenants paid rent for their farms. The surveyors were out again being carefully watched for any damage they might do to crops – for which compensation would be payable. Letters regarding areas and property to be taken were soon being distributed in the burghs and villages, and also to landowners and farmers in the countryside, ('Not at home, left with wife' was a record of one delivery).

Acts of Parliament gave railway companies sweeping powers to acquire land by compulsory purchase. It soon became apparent that being a lawyer by profession, or being on good terms with one, was advantageous when doing business with the NBR legal team. Compensation was possible for a variety of circumstances – there was the disturbance caused by construction works; cutting through fields and grazings caused 'inconvenience of intersection' and could prevent the watering of livestock, while disrupting paths and roads created 'circuitous access'. Nevertheless, the railway did get powers to cross certain roads 'on the level' and thereby save the expense of over bridges. As railways were seen as noisy and dirty

neighbours, amenity could be spoiled, and worse was 'the fact of compulsion' – there was little choice about having to sell. A curious compensation was for 'unexhausted manure' – on land taken by the railway that was capable of growing another crop or two. Out of any money received, landowners were expected to give their tenants 'an abatement of rent', plus recompense for temporary or permanent damage to their farms.

The transfer of land to the railway company might also involve the obligations attached to it – the school master's salary, minister's stipend and various local taxes, such as Cess and Feu Duties – all of which the NBR tried to avoid or minimise. However, it could not avoid Income Tax, Poors' Rates and Prison Assessments.

The NBR's lawyers had to be on the alert – for instance, at Falahill, where over 12 acres were acquired, the titles forbade any work or process likely to be 'a nuisance or obnoxious to the neighbourhood' taking place.

On the upland 'sheep walks', payments might amount to £80 per acre, whereas on arable land in the favoured valleys, it was almost three times as much. A rural cottage might be worth only £20 but country houses could be valued at over twenty times that sum and town prices could be even higher. Compensation issues for land and property could drag on for years and absorb a great deal of a railway company's time and money.

When the Parliamentary proceedings were in progress, it is interesting to speculate if Brunel and Miller actually met and exchanged views. Brunel had strong opinions on many matters, and if they did converse, he might have warned Miller about the 'extortionists', the land and property owners who were likely to stand in the way of the railway, and to extract as much compensation as possible. In some cases, such payments when totalled could practically have built the new railways, and the E&HR would come close to this predicament.

As a civil engineer John Miller is remembered today for his part in the Edinburgh & Glasgow Railway, and for a masterpiece completed in 1848 – the Ballochmyle viaduct on the Glasgow & South Western Railway. Its seven stone arches cross the deep valley of the River Ayr near Cumnock, and at 164ft (50.5m) it is the highest railway viaduct in Britain. By comparison, Miller's achievements with the Edinburgh & Hawick Railway have been largely forgotten. The Borders Railway revival will highlight his engineering skills in adapting an old waggonway, in designing a noble viaduct at what is now known as Lothianbridge, and in finding a route south through the valley of the meandering and temperamental Gala Water to reach the River Tweed and the Borders countryside.

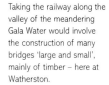

Taking the railway along the valley of the meandering Gala Water would involve the construction of many bridges 'large and small', mainly of timber – here at Watherston.

# Onwards to Hawick

The contracts for the Edinburgh & Hawick Railway were organised by parishes – the local administrative unit in the counties at that date – with the majority running from Newbattle to the Tweed Bridge east of Galashiels from where the Darnick, Minto and Newstead contracts continued south to Hawick. From the 1830s or even earlier, the main contractors had probably gained experience in making or maintaining roads for Turnpike Trusts. Knowledge about drainage, 'macadamised' road surfaces and bridge construction, could be turned to advantage for the formation of railways, or for road diversions around them. The principles of 'cut and fill'- taking earth from cuttings to form adjacent embankments – were already well known, but spoil banks were contentious – where would they be put and would they be permanent? If so, there was further compensation to be claimed by farmers.

Abbotsford estate, the prized possession of Sir Walter Scott, also figured in the compensation wrangles. By 1845 his son Walter, the second baronet, was the laird and a claim was entered for £1,977 to cover 5 acres, plus deterioration in amenity, the making of new accesses and the creation of embankments. These were to be 'covered with good soil to a depth of eight inches' and planted with mixed woodland. On this occasion, the actual mansion house at Abbotsford and its views were not affected by any railway works

Another influential landowner was James Pringle of Torwoodlee, who was also proprietor of the Buckholm estate. After a distinguished career in the Royal Navy, he retired as a Vice-Admiral. The Pringles were a long established Border family who had bought Torwoodlee in 1508. At a time when the Border country was often unsettled and violent, the location was strategic being high above a river gorge west of Galashiels. Altogether the Pringle lands ran to over 3,000 acres (1200ha). James Pringle looked for compensation for 'land take' and other matters, settling 'extrajudicially' after protracted arguments and interdicts that stopped work on the line. He received over £4,750 for 11 acres in August 1849 after complaining about the dumping of spoil, the unauthorised use of estate roads, damage to woodland and the removal of stone for the bridge to be built over the Tweed. He also expected the railway company to cover his legal costs.

The NBR fared better at Stow. The laird Andrew Mitchell, while warning about damage to the bed of the

This portrait of a young engineer with plan and top hat in hand also shows an embankment constructed on the 'cut and fill' principle. (Elton and Newby Collection, Darlington Borough Council)

river, gave ground for a road to the station. The company built a bridge across the river 'suitable for carriages and carts', constructed passages for his cattle and sheep beneath the line, and paid only £4,050 for 34 acres. Landowners were naturally protective of their interests. At Galabank, 'no Inn or Refreshment Rooms' were to be erected 'within half a mile of Galabank Inn', thus safeguarding a tenant's business and the laird's rent. Any hotel, tavern or residence was ruled out.

Lawsuits followed when dissatisfied proprietors raised actions in the Court of Session in Edinburgh when they discovered that the original plans had been modified. Railway Acts empowered companies 'to make or construct in, upon, across, under or over any Land or any Streets, Hills, Valleys, Roads, Rivers' and other features that stood in the way of their lines. The plans presented in Parliament allowed the E&HR to deviate from the route shown by as much as 100 yards on each side, to substitute cuttings for tunnels and to replace viaducts with embankments – the

The Pringles of Torwoodlee were Border lairds and Vice-Admiral James Pringle was an adversary of the Edinburgh & Hawick Railway. (John Peter)

The Edinburgh & Hawick Railway opened a station at Stow where it was well received by the landowner, Andrew Mitchell.

(R W Lynn Collection)

embankments, cuttings and tunnels were built by these tremendously powerful men with pick, spade, shovel and barrow'.

*– C Hamilton Ellis in 'The Pictorial Encyclopedia of Railways' (1968)*

Their reputation as ruffians and prize-fighters often caused fear in communities through which the new lines passed. In addition, hundreds of horses, moving tons of materials day after day, were the main earthmovers; they pulled primitive wagons over temporary tracks that contractors used before the 'permanent way' of the finished railway was laid. A navvy was capable of lifting 20 tons of spoil a day into such wagons, but had to supply his own shovel for the work.

Although the E&HR was part of a railway construction boom in Scotland, plenty of men were looking for employment. The potato crop in the Highlands and islands failed in the mid-1840s with deficiencies continuing into the 1850s. Although less catastrophic than in Ireland, (as there was less dependency on the potato as a staple food), there was localised destitution. The Free Church of Scotland assisted men to travel to work on railway projects in the Lowlands and some 3,000 did so. There local employment was boosted with better wages on offer than those on farms or estates. Tempting advertisements for 'masons, joiners, slaters, plumbers, plasterers, founders and smiths, etc' for the E&HR appeared in *The Scotsman* as the project advanced. Coal miners' expertise was put to good use in constructing tunnels. Initially, there were two small tunnels at Gorebridge, presumably to protect the gunpowder works there from sparks from engines, but there would be another two – the longest of 249yds at Bowshank, south of Stow, and a short one of 67yds at Torwoodlee, west of Galashiels;

Accommodation for navvies ranged from tolerable lodgings for contractors' key men to 'sod huts and shanties' for the majority. One of the worst was a sod cabin seen on the E&HR in April 1846; begun on a Saturday, it was occupied on the Monday. Only 27ft by 12ft, it housed 20

company only had to obtain certificates from the Board of Trade to do so. Some proprietors took exception to such adjustments – in one case the amount of land in dispute at Kirkhill near Newtongrange was only 'one thousandth part of an acre' where a cutting would be made less deep. Yet it was argued that this would be 'so destructive to the amenity of the place ... that no pecuniary damages would adequately compensate'. At Hawick, the magistrates were so displeased about the prospect of the line cutting through the town's Common Haugh that they prepared for a jury trial.

The contractors provided their own equipment and hired teams of navvies. These men came mainly from impoverished regions of Ireland and Scotland to work on railway schemes. The name was derived from the 'navigators' who had constructed the canals decades earlier. Navvies took justifiable pride in their strength and skill:

'Most of Britain's railways, with their immense

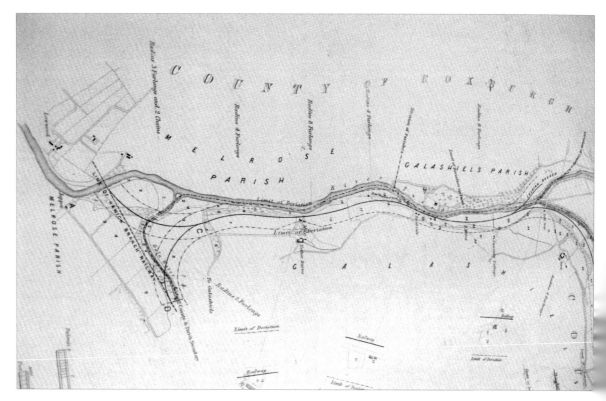

An excerpt from a North British Railway plan showing proposals for the Selkirk branch and the generous 'limits of deviation' for the construction of the line.

(Buccleuch Archives, Drumlanrig Castle)

This cutting near Halflawkiln, where excavators were at work in 2013, was originally dug out by navvies working in hazardous conditions to undercut the banks. (James Gildea, Network Rail)

This statue of a navvy stands at Gerrards Cross station as a tribute to the men who built Britain's railways. (John Peter)

Lothianbridge viaduct, with 23 arches over the valley of the River South Esk, the most impressive structure on the Edinburgh & Hawick Railway, is now an icon for the Borders Railway. (Whitehouse Studios, Network Rail)

Gorebridge was the scene of navvy riots, but nevertheless its station on the Edinburgh & Hawick Railway opened on 12 July 1847. (C J B Sanderson)

**Below:** Where once navvies led horses with carts to tip spoil and form the massive earthwork of Borthwick bank, the gradient of 1 in 75 is revealed when clearing the old track bed in 2013. Borthwick Castle is seen on the right.
(James Gildea, Network Rail)

**Below right:** Edinburgh's Cowgate in the Old Town was already poor and congested when it became home to Irish immigrants, many of whom looked for employment as navvies.
(John Peter)

people, often three to a bed. The back wall was a slope, saturated with water that trickled into the beds – yet the contractor charged a rent. The men had to provide their own food bargaining with local farmers for produce but some times helping themselves. When the poultry house at Torsonce Mains, near Stow, was burgled in June 1848, 'a large quantity of poultry' was carried off. The police went to 'the railway huts near Bowshank tunnel', found most of the birds and arrested four men.

Contractors might set up a store or 'tommy shop' ('tommy' being navvy slang for bread) and although the Truck Act of 1831 made it unlawful to pay wages in other than cash, this legislation did not apply to railway labourers. A Parliamentary Select Committee enquired into the shocking conditions endured by such navvies in 1846, but failed to produce any legislation. There were also navvy families with women and children in the camps; boys as young as eight were employed as 'greasers' to put tallow on the axles of contractors' wagons.

Where navvies gathered and much drink was taken, there could be trouble. Navvy camps thus called for policing.

Edinburghshire, Roxburghshire and Selkirkshire, the counties through which the railway would pass, had only rudimentary forces at the time – the NBR had to provide clothing for the Selkirk representatives. Railway police and an inspector were also recruited to maintain some order at the sites. Altogether, policing took almost £6,000 during the years of construction. It was a risky occupation with a serious riot reported in March 1846. Riots and bloodshed had marred the construction of the Edinburgh & Glasgow Railway and tensions could run high between navvies from different backgrounds who were tied to different contractors. The workforce on the E&HR was estimated to be some 3,000-4,000 men with 300-400 horses, the numbers being greater in summer when better weather allowed the line to advance more rapidly.

The key element in the Newbattle contract, held by Graham & Sandison, was the 23 arch viaduct to be constructed across the South Esk at Dalhousie. Their contract amounted to over £66,600, but also covered bridges and track work all the way to Gorebridge. The workforce of skilled tradesmen, such as masons, was

reported to be 'mainly two-thirds Scotchmen and one-third Englishmen'. An insight about the building of this mighty viaduct comes from the sale of the contractors' equipment in May 1849 when the project was complete. Cranes were crucial – a large quarry crane, 'nearly new', a building crane and two travelling cranes that would run on rails, were on site. There were long ladders, sets of block and tackle, grinding stones, sludge pumps and much timber, used for scaffolding and for formwork under the brick arches. In addition, there was stabling for twelve horses, a smithy and a wright's shop.

A contrast was the Borthwick contract of Wilson & Moore that involved much earth moving from a massive cutting to form a long embankment. Here most of the labourers were Irish. The Lowland Scots in the district were known for their anti-Irish prejudice – the steady influx of Irishmen into coal and ironstone mining, quarrying and brick making, had given rise to a persistent feeling that the Irish were stealing Scottish jobs and causing reductions in wages. This often led to open hostility and bigotry when taunts and fights on street corners could flare into rioting.

Navvies were relatively well paid – about 25p per day – but it did not help law and order that they got their wages monthly, a practice that only encouraged drunkenness and violence. Trouble on the E&HR began at Gorebridge where a pedlar complained to police that two watches had been filched from him by Irishmen in a public house. When two arrests were made and the supposed culprits lodged in a lock-up at Gorebridge, tempers flared. The Irish navvies determined to release their compatriots by night. They broke into the police station attacking and injuring two officers who were unable to resist the mob. The released prisoners were then led through Gorebridge in triumph.

Meanwhile, two other policemen – one railway and one county – had been instructed to visit public houses along the road southwards from Lothianbridge when the Irish mob was seen to approach. The constables tried to avoid detection but the cry went up, 'murder the police'. One escaped but the railway constable was so badly injured that he succumbed. Immediately a message was sent to Edinburgh for police reinforcements – parties of both county and city officers were despatched to scour the countryside for the Irish ringleaders, and thirteen prisoners were taken to Edinburgh.

This was the cue for the Scots and English working on

the viaduct contract, along with colliers from local pits, to settle old scores. At Lothianbridge, their number was 'fully 1,000 strong'. In a procession with bagpipes and bugle, and all armed with pick shafts and staves, they marched towards Fushiebridge. This was where Wilson & Moore's section began, but the Irish had already fled. Disappointed at not having the opportunity for a fight, the Lothianbridge men resolved to set fire to the Irish huts:

*'Beginning on Crichton Moor, they burned six or eight, then coming down to Borthwick Castle, they burned as many more … The demolition was only the work of a few minutes … constructed chiefly of wood and turf, and having large quantities of straw inside, the huts burned like tinder'.*

– The Scotsman, 4 March 1846

Although some forty police (both county and city) were present – the number of men from Lothianbridge was so overwhelming that the officers dared not interfere. Meanwhile, the navvies' womenfolk watched the huts burn, and once the roofs fell in, gathered up their few possessions and sat by the smoking ruins. Such an outrage showed that far stronger action was required, and a detachment (ironically) of Irish Dragoon Guards, a heavily armed cavalry troop, was sent out from Piershill Barracks in Edinburgh. With a sheriff in attendance, they rounded up nineteen of the arsonists.

Many of the Irish navvies driven off the line sought refuge in Edinburgh's Cowgate. From the 1750s, this district was

When navvies only received their wages monthly, inns became the focus for drunken brawls. Such an episode took place at Clovenfords when the Galashiels-Peebles branch was being constructed. (John Peter)

**Far left:** A view south at Tynehead, with the track bed scraped by 2013, shows where a tunnel was proposed but another long cutting was dug by hundreds of navvies. (James Gildea, Network Rail)

**Left:** The awkward site of Tynehead station where the premises were up the slope on the right. (TOPticl.com)

The deep cutting at Torwoodlee, looking south, another location with dangerous excavations on the Edinburgh & Hawick Railway, showing its tall bridge and rock drains. (Network Rail)

poor and overcrowded, but its closes were home to hundreds of Irish immigrants. (It earned the name 'Little Ireland', and later became the site of St Patrick's Roman Catholic Church, with Hibernian Football Club originating there in 1875). Once in the Cowgate, the navvies summoned their fellow-countrymen 'to pay the Scotchmen back with interest'. The following day the Irish force was ready and hundreds set out along the Dalkeith Road. However, a sheriff and police had got wind of the march and several miles from the city, the men were stopped. The sheriff 'remonstrated with them about the impropriety of their conduct' and advised them to turn back. Further arrests of arsonists were subsequently made and 'consultations' began with the contractors to try to prevent further violent confrontations.

This episode was not the only riot that took place on the E&HR. On the approach to Galashiels, land acquired at Comelybank and at Low Buckholmside was used for navvy camps. The Galashiels and Stow contracts together were worth over £134,000, but when the contractor went

bankrupt and left the contracts early in 1848, men were left without food or credit until money was sent from Edinburgh to pay their wages. Drunkenness then ensued and when police tried to maintain order, they were roughly handled. The citizens of Gala then came to their assistance and drove the navvies to their quarters – but once the police left, the navvies returned and smashed the windows in Low Buckholmside. When the county authorities were informed, the sheriff arrived and the Riot Act was read outside the Bridge Inn. With stones 'flying like hail', people were urged to stay in their homes. More police were summoned and, again with the assistance of Gala men, the riot was quelled.

The same bankruptcy caused an affray near Lauder where the owner of the local 'tommy shop' supplying the navvies, belonged to that village. With the contractor bankrupt, the owner shut the shop. When he refused to supply goods on credit, there was more rioting and dragoons had again to be summoned from Edinburgh to restore order.

Before work on the E&HR even began, there were worries about the line upsetting Sunday observance and weakening church discipline. At Greenhill in Ashkirk parish, the new railway was seen as disruptive when 'even the peaceful dwellings of the mountain shepherd' would be 'invaded by the worshippers of Mammon'. In April 1845 a letter in the name of 'the Sabbath Committee of the Free Synod of Merse & Tweeddale, Gattonside by Melrose', was presented against 'Sabbath Travel on the Edinburgh & Hawick Railway'. Arguments 'for and against' Sunday trains were debated at length by NBR shareholders at their meetings. These were times when religious controversy raged in Scotland, culminating in 1843 when over a third of the ministers and congregations broke away from the established Church of Scotland to set up their own 'Free Churches' – free from what was perceived as state interference.

For many years, the NBR directors continued to receive petitions from clergy against Sunday trains, but Royal Mail contracts obliged railway companies to run them.

With construction in progress, there were further disputes. On the lands of Crichton at Tynehead, a lengthy tunnel was first proposed allowing sheep 'to cross freely from one side of the railway to the other'. However, as cuttings were only about a twelfth of the cost of tunnels, a cutting was the eventual outcome. Then there was the matter of watercourses with workmen at Halflawhill 'tumbling the earth over a bank into a rivulet' flowing to the Water of Tyne, and dumping rubbish, a cause of potential flooding. A civil engineer was appointed to investigate whether building work was being carried out 'in a reckless, improper or unusual manner'.

Unforeseen benefits helped to move the project on; for example, an improved water supply was made from a borehole for Tynehead farm, plus ponds for livestock. New buildings arose, notably in Wilton parish near Hawick, where a new manse, school and schoolmaster's house were built to designs by George Smith of Edinburgh, the NBR's architect. These won lavish praise for the railway company for its co-operation.

A difficult portion of the E&HR was around Galashiels from Bowshank to the Tweed Bridge. From 2 June to 15 September 1848, there were several accidents, some being very serious and five fatalities in that stretch. Torwoodlee was notorious as it involved a deep cutting with a high overbridge, two bridges

Fisherrow harbour on he Firth of Forth where timber and other materials were imported to supply the Edinburgh & Hawick Railway's construction.

across rivers and a short tunnel. The method of making cuttings was fraught with danger. For a contract price, a team of men would take on an excavation. Preferring to work with a 'high face', they undercut the earth before allowing it to fall, with the intention of bringing down the greatest quantity of material in the shortest possible time – betting their survival on the unsupported weight staying up. Collapse of cuttings was a frequent occurrence. Yet a steam excavator had been patented in 1839 in the USA, but in Britain navvy labour was cheaper and more plentiful.

In advance of construction, foresters were employed to clear sites for the line, and hedges, shrubs and trees were later planted on embankments and cuttings to appease some land owners – the railway being obliged to maintain them in perpetuity. While 'invisible' wire fences were requested by some proprietors, on the Duke of Buccleuch's Dalkeith estate a solid masonry wall was preferred that still stands adjacent to the new track. Whatever the choice, by law the railway had to be enclosed throughout its length.

As with the Borders Railway, materials for the E&HR typically came from the north end of the line, where it was essential that the new railway would be 'up and running' as soon as possible. With the track bed formed, the line opened to Gorebridge on 12 July 1847. To reach that point the new viaduct across the South Esk at Lothianbridge had been completed. Rails came from suppliers as far apart as the West of Scotland and North East England. Sleepers were imported principally from Memel on the Baltic through Fisherrow and Leith, but the supply chain was upset by the scarcity of lighters for offloading the timber on the Forth. A sufficient quantity of cast iron chairs and spikes, together with thousands of wooden keys to hold the rails in place, had to be carted to sites and many 'trenails' or wooden pegs, were also used.

In the interest of economy, some bridges carrying the tracks over the Gala Water and other streams had stone piers and abutments supporting timber structures, but others were entirely wooden. As far as possible, the Gala Water was respected as a fishing river, but it was proposed to divert it to suit the railway at Fountainhall. With hard winters being experienced, requests came for ice fenders for the bridges at Bowshank and at Bowland.

The E&HR soon had cash flow problems. As consulting engineer, John Miller was to receive £300 a quarter and be responsible for the supply of points and switches. However, by December 1846, he was owed £2,350 in fees. Possibly as a sweetener, the company then paid £12 to an optician for his spectacles – and his portrait shows him wearing them. Like the contractors, he had to be content with bills at 4 months. In June 1848, he was to receive £8,400 to settle his accounts. A year later, he was again requesting payment, but was given preference shares for £1,000 with the promise of cash in the course of the month.

An early view of Eskbank & Dalkeith station with its timber footbridge, clock and telegraph office.
(R W Lynn Collection)

**Above:** Only the north side platform survives at Melrose as a road now occupies the former south side area.

**Right:** At Eskbank a succession of over bridges was a feature of the long cutting on the Edinburgh & Hawick Railway. The track became a cycle and pedestrian way.

(Timon Rose)

**Below:** When contructed, the Lothianbridge viaduct had open piers giving it a light appearance but these were subsequently infilled with masonry.

**Above two:** At Melrose station used by visitors to Abbotsford and the abbey, an elaborate 'Jacobean' style was chosen for a building that has now found other uses.

The handsome station building at Eskbank & Dalkeith was probably a John Miller design to please influential local landowners.

When Miller was away attending to other railway business in Ayrshire, the project was taken forward by James Bell of the NBR, with resident engineer George Glennie and assistants. Vehicles were hired for the engineers and reveal their status – a barouche taking four persons for the principals, a two-seater chaise for inspectors, and a phaeton (described as fast but dangerous) for the young assistants.

By October 1846, an investment of over £518,000 had already been made in the E&HR and it was costing 20 per cent more than Miller's estimate. While opening stations as soon as possible would bring much needed revenue, these were reckoned to cost about £1,000 a piece to build and set up. So stations on the E&HR would be limited in number and of a basic description. The simple stone-built station at Burnmouth on the East Coast route was proposed as a model and thus stone was used if available locally. Stow station shows that influence. Galashiels station was a handsome building designed by John Miller himself, whose hand may also be detected today in some surviving station buildings.

The NBR's declared intention was to avoid 'useless expense in ornamental works' but one station would be different – Melrose. This was seen as a prelude to visits to the ruined abbey and to Abbotsford, Sir Walter Scott's mansion. (In 1844, the Scott Monument had just been completed in the centre of Edinburgh; this was accessed by Waverley Bridge adjacent to the railway station that would share that name). Melrose station, described as 'Scottish Jacobean' in style, was close to the Abbotsford estate and it was by far the most elaborate example on the NBR in the 1840s. Although bereft of its railway, the main building is intact but the south platform is now under the A6091, a result of road improvements since the closure of the Waverley Route.

From Melrose, the E&HR swung round the flank of the Eildon Hills to continue to Newtown (as St Boswells was first known on the line). The intention was to place a station on the green there, but this was the site of the annual St Boswell's Fair. It was also opposed by the Buccleuch Hunt whose kennels overlooked the green site. The railway was thus located further west and the station, with a sloping access, was built a mile away at 'Newtown'. The line then went over undulating country by the wayside stations of Belses and Hassendean to Hawick. There the first station was located on an open area at the north end of the town – to reduce expensive claims for compensation for land and property in the burgh.

In June 1847 Captain J. Coddington, Royal Engineers, Inspector of Railways, paid a visit to 'Part of the Hawick Line, as far as Gore Bridge, including alterations and improvements of the Dalkeith Tramway'. Accompanied by the resident engineers Glennie and Jardine and the locomotive superintendent Robert Thornton, the tour began at 'Niddry Junction' described as 'an important spot' where four sets of rails met – from Portobello, Musselburgh, Dalkeith and St Leonards. The captain found the junction sadly deficient. Part was 'impassable', part had no rails, and an embankment was short of the proper height. Furthermore, there were no signals as the engineer 'had yet to decide what to choose'.

Despite this inauspicious start, there were some improvements to commend. Towards Dalkeith, sharp curves had been rounded off with the ruling radius revised to 30 chains – although there were some curves that were tighter. The gradients were thought 'very severe' at 1 in 70 for over

The abandoned Fountainhall station where the Edinburgh & Hawick Railway opened on 4 August 1848.

8 miles from Hardengreen up to Falahill. With such curves and steep inclines, the captain considered the line would require 'great caution in the working'. The cuttings and embankments in 'strong hard clay' were judged 'considerable', the former being as much as 42 ft deep and the latter over 55ft high. So far 'no slips of any consequence had shown themselves', though slippage of embankments had in fact occurred at Gorebridge and at Borthwick where extra timber for reinforcements had been bought.

There were sixteen bridges over roads. All had freestone abutments and brick arches but the captain did not like the 'obliquity' of some of these. One was as much as '12 feet out of the square'. As for the four bridges made under the railway up to Gorebridge, one was entirely of ashlar and the others had cast iron superstructures. These had been tested with an engine loaded to 30 tons crossing at 20 miles an hour to measure the deflection, which the captain 'double checked' himself with another locomotive.

As to viaducts, the single arch over the North Esk near Dalkeith, dating from 1829-31, had been adapted from the old tramway. For double track, a timber platform projecting 5 ft over the masonry at each side with handrails 'for the workmen to stand aside upon when a train passes' had been built. There were checkrails along the whole structure to prevent derailments.

The second viaduct was a new build – the structure of 23 arches over the South Esk at Lothianbridge where the piers and abutments were 'of solid freestone ashlar of the best quality' with arches of brick. Founded on 'solid red sandstone rock', the tallest pier at 54 ft stood in the river. There was a curve in the viaduct over this pier, and 'owing to its great height and the obliquity of the strain upon it', a slight crack had appeared, 'extending from the level course downwards about 8 feet'. As a precaution the base had been lengthened and the pier 'hooped with timber beams and iron straps'. (The accounts for the E&HR show that £190 was paid for bolts and straps for Lothianbridge). As there was 'not another shake or flaw of any kind', the captain considered that the structure was 'perfectly secure'. At that date, all the piers had a 'hollow central interval' adding greatly to 'the beauty and light appearance of the viaduct'. (This was a design feature also followed in Brunel's Wharncliffe viaduct on the Great Western Railway's main line).

Although the E&HR was sanctioned as a single line, the captain found that it was already being constructed as double track with rail of '70lbs to the yard fixed with cast-iron chairs, wooden keys and sleepers of Baltic red wood'. The railway was only laid and ballasted to Dalhousie Mains, being incomplete towards Gorebridge. The captain noted that 'considerable difficulty' had been experienced in taking

The modest Bowland station which was a temporary terminus for the Edinburgh & Hawick Railway in 1848.

the project forward while 'maintaining the old horse-traffic with trains every two hours'. As the former Dalkeith Railway was now fit for the 'safe employment of locomotives', the horse traffic should be stopped, and the E&HR be permitted to open the section from St Leonards to Dalhousie. The removal of the embargo on steam locomotives was unwelcome by some proprietors; Sir John Hope argued that they must on no account come nearer his mansion house than 800 yards, while engines should be kept quiet with 'no blowing off when standing, starting or stopping'. The confusing Niddrie Junction and the extension to Gorebridge would require another visit.

The prospect of a station at Gorebridge was already having an effect on property values. In May 1847, a substantial house was for sale, consisting 'of Two Flats ... Seven Rooms and Three Closets with the Garden behind ...in the immediate vicinity of the proposed Station' – this would give 'easy access from Edinburgh'. Such property could be expected to increase in value, and 'form a desirable place of Business or Summer Residence'.

In step with the NBR's aspirations, where the E&HR parted from the East Coast route, the name 'Hawick Junction' had appeared. (It was later re-named Portobello East Junction). The signalman Robert Skeldon set up a

system of weights and wires that allowed the signals to be worked from his box, a labour and cost saving innovation. This won awards and is an early example of 'remote control' on railways. Otherwise, the captain was satisfied that the stations on the E&HR had signals, the switches 'of patent form, with levers and balance weights' were in order; staff from the old line was available to run the trains, and the company had sufficient rolling stock for the initial operation.

With the construction of the line advancing southwards, storekeepers were employed and a waste book kept (revealing the NBR's 'waste not want not' policies). Timber and wire for fences were delivered, yards were prepared with loading banks and sidings, water supplies were arranged for locomotives and a well dug at Fountainhall station. Attention had already turned to painting bridges, carting tiles and placing mileposts. A quarry was rented for stone and locomotives hired from the parent NBR at £5 a day to spread ballast, commonly just engine ash, on the track bed. Wagon turntables and water columns were also ordered.

Nearing completion, the equipping and furnishing of the stations began. There were purchases of everything from inkstands to ticket cases with padlocks, from weighing machines to keys for securing the premises. The Carron Company supplied grates.

Thomas Edmondson & Son, providers to railway companies of small card tickets that could be numbered to prevent fraud, was contacted. The station clocks, worth £75 in total, came from Robert Bryson of Edinburgh, a chronometer maker with an interest in mathematics. He had concerns that tradesmen suffered from a lack of mathematical instruction and would benefit from technical education. In 1821 a pioneering initiative began for what would become the Watt College, subsequently maturing into Heriot Watt University where Halls of Residence bear Bryson's name. For many country folk, his station clocks would be the first timepieces they ever saw.

A timetable was published for the opening of a temporary terminus at Bowland based on Standard Railway Time. This essential measure put paid to 'local time' and had an immediate effect on communities throughout Britain. 'Railway Time' was introduced in 1840 following a compilation of company timetables by George Bradshaw. A year later, his monthly guides first appeared and soon a railway timetable became known as a 'Bradshaw'. From just 8 pages in 1841, this information for passengers grew to over a thousand pages, including maps and illustrations, by 1898.

There was however a pressing problem about completing the line – lack of finance. Railways were the most complex and expensive organisations to construct and to operate that had ever been seen. They almost invariably cost much more than had been estimated and the E&HR proved no exception. In February 1848 came a troubled letter from Miller to request advertisements for contractors to complete the works 'from near Bowshank to Melrose'. The engineer was instructed to get estimates for a tunnel at Bowshank – in place of the one proposed at Tynehead. It was hoped that coal would be found at Bowshank. Urgent measures were taken to hold down costs, and suppliers of rails and of sleepers were asked to reduce deliveries.

As for 'the Dunse, Kelso and other branches', the directors hesitated about advancing any of these. Although the temporary station at Bowland was approved, extra works at Galashiels were delayed and a subscription for a footbridge over the river there was refused. The directors were warned not to do anything that might 'endanger the great retaining wall at Ladhope' when attempting to squeeze the line through between steep slopes and the Gala Water, but there were soon issues over the stability of a nearby chapel.

There was also the need for locomotives to work the new branch and so orders were placed in October 1846 with the NBR's regular supplier, R & W Hawthorn of Newcastle. On the list were eight passenger engines, all 2-4-0s of a new design costing £2,375 each, while eight heavy goods engines with smaller wheels were also ordered. Hawthorns were to be paid in instalments and in March 1848 a bill for £3,000 was aimed at keeping them content. There was soon dissatisfaction with the engines because a year later workshops were set up at Hawick with a crane, tools and materials for repairing them. The mechanical weaknesses of the locomotives running on what proved to be a tough line became increasingly apparent. When their deficiencies were better understood, they became candidates for rebuilding, a solution that the NBR used for many years, and some even survived into the 1900s.

Coal wagons and timber trucks were bought for the expected freight traffic. In 1844 at its outset the NBR had 230 goods vehicles, including cattle trucks and horseboxes, but by 1849 this had grown to just over 1,600 – indicating the significance of freight for the company. With an eye to business, a temporary loading bank was made at Whitehill for St Boswell's Fair, an annual focus for trade in horses and cattle. A curiosity sanctioned by the directors was 'a safety van for the conveyance of gunpowder' from Gorebridge. These vehicles were constructed of metal lined with wood and were marshalled carefully between wagons that were either empty or carrying non-flammable materials – and they were kept at a safe distance on sidings. The loads were classified as 'dangerous goods' but 'common carrier' legislation obliged railways to take them. To encourage even more freight, sheds to protect goods in transit, such as lime,

**NORTH BRITISH RAILWAY**

**LANGLEE & SYMINGTON**

**TORWOODLEE & THORNILEE**

*AND*

**RINK & SELKIRK**

**BRANCHES**

A range of branch lines projected by the North British Railway was delayed by lack of funds and downturns in the economy. (Buccleuch Archives, Drumlanrig Castle)

were considered – but deferred on cost grounds, as were houses for surfacemen. The cutbacks continued with engineers being warned to limit the number of wagon turntables purchased.

In May 1848 Parliament approved the alteration in gradients beyond Fushiebridge and the levels at Galashiels, but Miller cautioned about the consequences of 'retardation of the works' as the company might face claims for damages with the 'prolongation' taking the railway beyond the statutory time for completion. Therefore, the Hawick branch should be tackled 'with as much expedition as the financial affairs of the Company will allow'.

With the temporary terminus at Bowland agreed, 'Agents, Porters etc for the various Stations about to be opened on the Hawick Branch' were recruited together with pointsmen and watchmen. 'Agents' were in fact stationmasters and the NBR expected them not only to drum up business locally (usually sales of coal) but also 'to find security of £100 for their intromissions'. Porters' pay was cut from two shillings to one shilling (10p) a week, 'tips' from passengers hopefully making up their earnings. There was no surprise that the proposed fares on the new branch would be 'the maximum the Act allows'. The speed of trains was limited to just 20mph.

In June 1848, the NBR's services on the 'Dalkeith & Hawick Branch' were being advertised. Musselburgh and Portobello were also mentioned, having formerly been

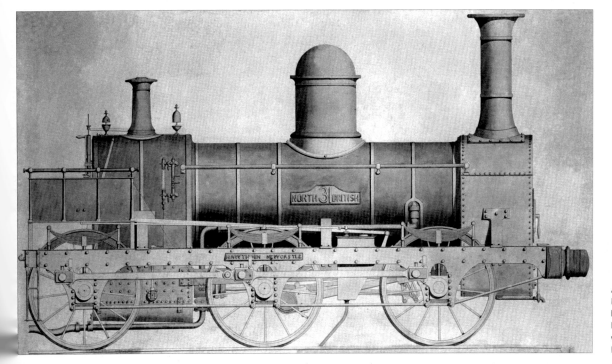

A North British Railway locomotive of the 1850s, built by R&W Hawthorn, Newcastle, of a type that worked on the Edinburgh & Hawick Railway. (Glen Collection)

The North British Railway had gunpowder vans for Gorebridge traffic, probably with a wood lining similar to this example under restoration at the Ffestiniog Railway.

The directors of the Edinburgh & Hawick Railway were warned to take care not to damage the Ladhope Wall or property on the way into Galashiels.

served by the Edinburgh & Dalkeith Railway. To Bowland, it took 1 hour 35 minutes from Edinburgh by three trains out and back on weekdays, with 1st, 2nd and 3rd class on offer. On Sundays there were just two trains, probably run as requirement of the Royal Mail – one from Edinburgh at 9am and from Bowland at 8.45am, the first of these having 4th class vehicles. Arrangements were made to liaise with coach proprietors to convey passengers to Galashiels, Melrose, St Boswells, Kelso and Hawick – in connection with the 9am and 4.30pm trains from Edinburgh – an early example of 'integrated transport'.

As the passengers were mostly unacquainted with rail travel, some instructions were given about this new mode of transport as there were 'Regulations' to be observed. People were 'booked conditionally on there being room in the Train and Class of Carriage'. Tickets were 'granted' and passengers were warned to get their tickets 'at least five minutes before the time marked as the trains may start to that extent sooner'. They were requested to look after their luggage and 'strongly recommended to have their name and destination marked on each package'. Each class had its own luggage allowance. Tickets for children were much as today, children under three

years travelling 'free' and under twelve for 'half fare'. Where private carriages were conveyed, parties 'riding inside' had to pay 1st class fares and servants 2nd class ones; it was pointed out that 'horses are not taken by Express Trains'. Smoking in carriages and at stations was forbidden 'under a penalty by Act of Parliament'. Refreshments rooms were mentioned, presumably at the NBR's Edinburgh station, and parcels could be forwarded to all parts of England. A transport revolution was beginning in the Borders, and for the hard-pressed E&HR, some revenue would accrue from ticket sales and ease its cash flow problems. For Borderers, the days of tedious journeys on stagecoaches over rough turnpike roads to Edinburgh, or further a-field, were over.

Inevitably, there were adverse effects for some businesses when the railway opened. An advertisement appeared in 'The Scotsman' in August 1848 for the sale of 'very superior horses, carts, harness etc' the property of the Edinburgh-Hawick carrier. The horses were described as 'very powerful and good roadsters', worthy of the attention of brewers, and mill masters. Although the line had not yet been completed to Hawick, it would come soon enough and a carrier would be unable to compete with the new railway.

The Act of 1845 required the electric telegraph to be installed on the E&HR. When the Electric Telegraph Company offered its services, the directors at first declined, but negotiations continued. Subsequently, they suggested that the wires could be set up on an experimental basis though it was then disclosed that 'the Patentee', would have to pay for the installation all the way to Hawick. The practice was for the telegraph companies to pay rent to the railway for the use of the trackside for their poles and wires.

Meantime, demands for compensation payments kept coming. The Marquis of Lothian asked for compensation for the interruption to his coal traffic arising from the construction works. In January 1849 a jury awarded Admiral Pringle £1,375 for ground at Buckholm. At Torwoodlee, money had to be found for a new bridge and road to the Admiral's Ryehaugh. Worse, a new timber bridge over the line had collapsed and the resident engineer was told forthwith to give 'careful personal inspection to all the works in progress'.

The turnpike roads and bridges were taking punishment from 'heavy carriages', including timber, rail, and stone going to the construction sites while bricks in quantity were being carted by road to line Bowshank tunnel. So the Turnpike Trustees looked for money to make proper repairs, 'metalled according to Mr McAdam's mode, and blinded with pit or river gravel'.

The NBR's astute company secretary, lawyer Charles Davidson, used various techniques to help the E&HR cope with the cash flow problem. One was to pay in instalments, or delay settling accounts for as long as possible. So debts incurred in 1848 were in some instances not paid until 1850. Another was to dispute the quality of goods supplied, for example, rejecting rail and sleepers, even although that might affect completion. Meanwhile, directors went cap in hand to as many banks as possible looking for an injection of funds with money 'available on directors' bills at 6½ per cent'. They also pressed shareholders to respond promptly to calls for yet more cash. Creditors were fended off with quantities of preference stock. As a last resort, there was Miller's strategy of 'retardation' – putting off the completion of a section of the line for some months especially track laying, ballasting or station construction.

A painting by Robert Sanderson shows a harvest field in the Lothians close to a small colliery – such enterprises received a boost by the opening of the Edinburgh & Hawick Railway. (Science & Society Picture Library)

Eventually the E&HR had to apply to Parliament to increase its capital – and £600,000 was then permitted.

In 1845 Miller had been sanguine about the competence and solvency of contractors for the E&HR. However, in August 1846 floods had overwhelmed the NBR's new East Coast line to Berwick-on-Tweed, destroying bridges. In 1849, as engineer for that line, Miller was called to account by the NBR directors, but blame was laid on the contractors and their lack of experience in railway construction. However, Miller's reputation had been questioned. By this stage he was only making occasional visits to the E&HR, being much occupied between 1846-50 with another major project, the Glasgow, Dumfries & Carlisle Railway through Nithsdale (this would become part of the Glasgow & South Western Railway). With the tracks about to reach Hawick, from 5 October 1849 Miller chose to resign 'active charge' of the E&HR. From then on, he would act only as a consulting engineer 'if the directors desired it' and further works would be left to resident engineers and assistants.

Regarding the NBR branch lines for which powers had been taken in the Act of 1846, Miller was prepared to join colleagues in a consortium of 'Blyth, Jopp and Miller' that offered to supervise the completion of the branches for £2,000. Benjamin Hall Blyth was an experienced consulting engineer and had been the mastermind for Monkland Railways, and Charles Jopp, a senior engineer in the employment of the NBR, would be remembered as a designer of impressive viaducts. Their offer was declined.

Having drawn up plans for over 1,500 miles of railway while in practice, Miller's finances must have come good as he retired a wealthy man aged just 45 to a grand house at Polmont; he then purchased two country estates and in 1868 became a Liberal MP for Edinburgh.

In spite of the boom in railway promotions and construction in the 1840s, the decade would be remembered as the 'Hungry Forties'. A letter to the board asked if 'the unemployed poor in Galashiels' could find employment on the NBR. When the railway did open there

Heriot, with staggered platforms on either side of a level crossing, was a simple station that also opened on 4 August 1848. (R W Lynn)

The Leaderfoot viaduct on the Berwickshire Railway was an expensive investment in yet another North British branch line.

John Miller's design for Galashiels station was an attractive addition to the town, a building that has been sadly lost. (National Archives of Scotland)

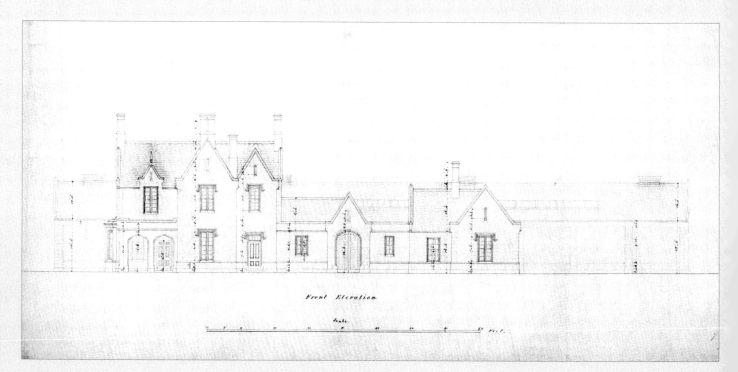

*Front Elevation*

in February 1849, and to Hawick in November of that year, there were no ceremonial openings, there were no flags flying or bands playing. Such frivolities meant expense. A dinner at Melrose for the directors took place and there was a testimonial to John Learmonth. This had been a shareholder's suggestion, and his choice was a portrait and a piece of silver plate 'suitably inscribed'.

Nevertheless, just when some revenue from traffic was beginning, there came another financial blow for the NBR – Captain Scott, a key land owner in Galashiels, had gone to arbitration over compensation for amenity and agricultural damage caused by the new railway. To the consternation of the NBR directors, he was awarded £8,233 in February 1850. Overgenerous awards, for those 'suffering at the hands of the railway', were given by the establishment to each other as the judiciary and landowners were often closely linked. The total expense of land take and compensation had now reached £189, 570 – almost 40 per cent of the entire cost of the projected line.

Unrelenting economy would have to be the way forward for the management of the E&HR. However, pay cuts for employees resulted in enginemen threatening to withdraw their labour in April 1850. The directors resisted combinations of employees, with jail terms for those who 'failed to give notice of intent to leave their work'. The episode would leave a residue of bitterness in industrial relations for the NBR.

By 1850 some better news was coming for the NBR's border investments. The Kelso branch opened on 7 June 1850 providing a route east from Newtown St Boswells to

The First Edition 6-inch Ordnance Survey map of 1858-9 for Galashiels shows the station and extensive goods yard that were developing in the burgh. (National Library of Scotland Map Room)

In 1854 the opening of a branch from Galashiels to Selkirk and the availability of coal led to its mills being sited close to the railway yards. (R W Lynn)

districts of fertile arable land in the Merse. A North Eastern Railway branch from Tweedmouth via Sprouston was met a few miles east of Kelso, although that town's station was at Maxwellheugh, south of the River Tweed. In 1850 Galashiels station earned a surplus of over £4,000 and goods receipts were rising. Coal was emerging as the NBR's biggest source of revenue and so weighing stations were set up at Niddrie and Falahill in addition to Tranent – by 1851 these were handling almost a quarter of a million tons a year. Even so, there was dissatisfaction among the English shareholders who feared that the company was over-extending itself. Loans were still being negotiated in the name of the directors and unease was caused by the very large sums being spent on Parliamentary Bills, legal costs, share purchases and interest payments. In 1852 John Learmonth was ousted as chairman.

With NBR funds being scarce, communities keen to have a rail connection had to raise the capital to construct a branch, and only then would the NBR make arrangements to work the line. Construction costs had to be held down too. When the Peebles branch from the E&HR at Eskbank came to be made, it was 'on the cheap principle'; it then ran its own services with hired NBR engines and carriages for several years. By this means a rash of branches was authorised – Selkirk-Galashiels in 1854, Jedburgh-Roxburgh in 1855 and Galashiels-Peebles in 1861. The following year, the Berwickshire Railway from Dunse to Newstead near St Boswells was sanctioned.

Captain Tyler of the Board of Trade, making an inspection of the Selkirk branch in April 1865, wrote:

*'The permanent way is of a light description and the rails are not fished. The gradients are severe and the curves sharp, and altogether the line is not fitted for heavy traffic or high speeds'.*

Foregoing fishplates to hold lengths of rail together was not only 'cheap' but also dangerous. On the opening day, the platform was a pile of sleepers covered with earth and a 'primitive shanty' served as the station building. This was reached down a steep hill from the town. Nevertheless, stations attracted trade and both Selkirk and Newtown St Boswells soon had entrepreneurs running 'Railway Hotels' beside them.

On the NBR's branches, there were construction problems in crossing the Tweed, notably at the 19-arch Leaderfoot viaduct where abutment weaknesses required iron hoops. The branches had their navvy troubles too. On 18 July 1853, with St Boswell's Fair in full swing, fights broke out between local men and navvies working on the line. Troops had to be summoned from Edinburgh to restore order. Another episode of drunken rioting occurred at Clovenfords during the building of the Peebles branch.

Although embarking on so many branches was seen as 'ruinous' to the NBR's finances, by June 1866, it was possible for passengers to travel from Galashiels to Peebles by rail, and going either east or west, north or south in the Borders, NBR metals had been laid. In addition, a remarkably even distribution of small stations and sidings had formed at convenient distances 'out and back' for a horse and cart to access railway yards in the countryside. The Railway Age had indeed come to the Borders.

Once the Edinburgh & Hawick Railway opened to Galashiels, its presence was noted in this sketch and the smoky chimneys of mills and houses showed the use of coal.
(Robert Hall, History of Galashiels)

# Bound for Carlisle

A welcome addition to income for railway companies was the Royal Mail. This was already being conveyed on the NBR's Edinburgh & Hawick line – but trains carrying such consignments were expected to travel at 25 miles per hour. The company had a problem 'attended with inconvenience and expense' that on the sinuous 8 mile descent from Middleton Muir down Borthwick Bank to Dalhousie Mains, a 15 mile per hour speed limit continued in force. This slowed up the time taken by trains on the long run of 53 miles from Hawick. The restriction had been imposed by Parliament in the 1845 Act when the intention was to make the Edinburgh & Hawick Railway a single line as this 'soothed anxieties' about an incline of 1 in 75 with curves of only 20 chains radius. However, from the outset John Miller had ensured that 'a double line of rails' was laid and the curves eased.

So in September 1853, Captain Wynn, RE, of the Railway Inspectorate, was sent to investigate. He found the line double tracked throughout and the curves ' much more favourable', none now being less than 30 chains radius. Furthermore, the outside rail on all the curves had been 'elevated to meet the effects of centrifugal force' – an early reference to 'cant' in permanent way matters. (This technique had not been mentioned by either Brunel or Miller at the Bill Committee proceedings in 1845). The inspector reported:

*I travelled down the incline with an engine running tender foremost at speed varying from thirty to forty miles per hour, and at that speed and under the undesirable circumstances of pushing the tender in front, I passed perfectly smoothly over the curves'.* – Geo. Wynn, Captain, Royal Engineers

He trusted that the directors would take 'every precaution to have the line maintained in proper working order' and that the Board of Trade would therefore give authority to raise the speed to 25 miles an hour.

The new E&HR was generally welcomed. The trains moved lime and fertiliser for agriculture (guano imported from South America became popular) and livestock to new markets from wayside stations such as Belses and Hassendean. The days of driving animals would be numbered. The line brought a new mobility to the Borders, not least to women. The exceptions were the snobs who bemoaned the fact that railways were bringing together 'such an objectionable mix of people'. Among the passengers were the fishwives from Fisherrow, who could now take their creels of 'caller herrin' to Galashiels, thereby introducing fresh seafood to Borders tables. A report by the Board of Trade revealed that over 70 per cent of Scottish passengers travelled Third Class – they seemed to put 'value for money' before comfort.

By 1855 the new chairman of the NBR was Richard Hodgson, MP for Berwick and a Border squire. He was energetic and committed to the company. Initially, remarkable improvements in performance and revenue were achieved under his regime, with the assistance of a capable general manager Thomas Rowbotham and locomotive superintendent William Hurst. That year William H Charlton of Hesleyside, another MP and a Northumberland landowner, cut the first sod for the Border Counties Railway. This line diverged from the Newcastle & Carlisle line near Hexham, following the North Tyne valley to a coalfield at Plashetts in the Cheviot Hills. The two railway chairmen would find common ground for their ambitions in the economic boom of the mid-1850s.

Hodgson viewed the Caledonian Railway as the arch enemy and his policy soon became clear – to neutralise and outflank that company. During his rule, described as resolute and remorseless but unscrupulous, the NBR mileage increased dramatically from a 58-mile main line on the East Coast, with some branches, to a system with 781 miles of

Hassendean station has found a new use as a residence but retains its railway ambience as the restored veranda shows.
(R W Lynn)

## THE WAVERLEY ROUTE
### WITH BRANCHES AND OTHER LINES

This map of the Waverley Route shows the relationship of the line to the Border and the numerous stations south of Riccarton Junction on the way to Carlisle. The link via the Border Counties Railway with Hexham is also shown.
(Ian Allan Publishing)

than Whitrope at 1,006ft. The CR also proposed a branch to Canonbie where there were coal measures. Both were seen as hostile intents. In response, the NBR produced a plan for its own double track line down Liddesdale via Newcastleton to Carlisle. The NBR was not going to accept being 'shut up within its own threshold at Hawick'. Among the Border towns, only Langholm backed the CR scheme. Hodgson, a Tory, went on the campaign trail summoning allies not only from the other Border towns but also from the Lothians and from influential organisations in Edinburgh. In August 1858 a lavish dinner was held in his honour at Hawick when special trains brought hundreds of supporters of the proposed Carlisle line.

Behind the scenes, efforts were made to come to terms with the Caledonian Railway with joint management and free interchange of traffic suggested, but there was no response from the CR to Hodgson's proposals. Accordingly, the NBR announced its intentions for the Border Union Railway, its own Liddesdale line, which would make it a 'main line company'. It was a bold move, but many shareholders were less sure and some commentators saw little point in it.

In 1859 John Miller appeared as a witness before the Bill Committee for the Border Union Railway. The route would be yet another with sharp reverse curves, tedious steep gradients, bridges, viaducts and a long tunnel, all making it expensive to construct, to operate and to maintain. South of Hawick, it would run through sparsely populated uplands of wind swept 'shanks', cut by 'sykes' or narrow valleys. Here sheep grazed and revenue potential was very limited, although there might be workable coal amid the hills. However, this was not a line driven by economic necessity but by railway politics – a means of checkmating the Caledonian company. For most NBR directors, buoyed up and cajoled by Hodgson as chairman, this was the game plan and a matter of corporate pride. The Act for the Border Union Railway received the Royal Assent on 21 July 1859.

The first sod was cut with due ceremony by Mrs Hodgson at Hawick on 7 September. Special trains were run to the town from the north. It was a day of ceremony with bands playing when civic leaders, masons, police, railway officials, clergy, engineers and navvy representatives marched in procession. A luncheon with many toasts for the success of the project followed, much being made of its expected benefits. In due course, tours were organised from Hawick to allow townsfolk to view the construction in progress.

There were nine contracts for the 50 miles of line through the difficult terrain of the Southern Uplands. They varied in length from over 6 miles for the Hawick, Hermitage and Penton contracts to only 3½ miles at Newcastleton and Riccarton. Soon camps of wooden huts, stables for horses, smithies, offices, and equipment appeared. On the Hawick contract, the line left the old station site round curves to reach a new station close to the River Teviot. Two viaducts were necessary to take the line out of Hawick – on the Teviot and the Slitrig, the latter stream being diverted in part. Construction camps were set up at Shankend, and further south at Whitrope, with others at Riccarton, Hermitage and Newcastleton on the way to Carlisle.

When 'roaring pay nights' brought navvies into Hawick, the town was exposed to drunkenness and violence on an unprecedented scale with the police unable to cope. The Temperance Movement had been growing in strength from the 1830s – the railways assisting the spread of its

track and equipment estimated to be worth over £22 million. However, rapid expansion came at a damaging cost.

At the commencement of the NBR in 1845, the Bill contained a reference to powers for an extension from Hawick to Carlisle. As the Board of Trade did not approve of this route, the clause was removed but it was not forgotten. A route had been surveyed and, as early as 1848, a 'Carlisle Extension scrip issue' to raise funds was discussed but the idea was dropped. Carlisle was becoming a 'mecca' for railway companies, for their routes and trade, beginning in 1836 with the opening of the Newcastle & Carlisle Railway.

In 1857 a Carlisle & Hawick line, along Teviotdale, put forward by the Caledonian Railway, represented a worrying intrusion into territory that the NBR considered part of its fiefdom. The Teviotdale route, through Langholm, would have been an easier choice, only topping 849ft – much less

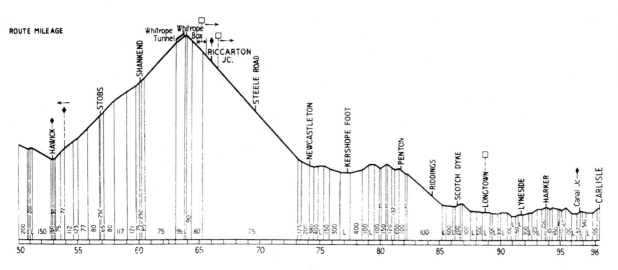

The gradient profile of the Waverley Route from Hawick to Carlisle showing the ascents south from Hawick and from Newcastleton north to the summit at Whitrope. (BR Scottish Region)

message of sobriety – but there was little evidence of this in Hawick. Although licensing laws had been passed limiting the hours when alcohol could be sold, the burgh was split between those who decried the navvies' excesses and those who profited from them. As alternatives to drinking, concerned citizens organised evening concerts and soirées for the men. However, illegal shebeens flourished and whisky from illicit stills up in the Cheviot Hills found a ready market in the camps.

Three wild winters were followed by two wet summers. The longer the project took, the greater the outlays became. By April 1861, an inspection report highlighted the multiple problems 'with Works, Cuttings and Embankments' on the Border Union Railway. Starting with the Hawick contract, the Slitrig viaduct, built of 'greywacke, rough rubble, and somewhat in haste', had a cracked pier, the facing stones were disintegrating, and a locomotive would shortly test it 'rather severely'. The masonry of the Barnes bridge near Stobs was shrinking and cracking – the weather being blamed. Nevertheless, as the contractor had the advantage of being near roads and the town of Hawick for supplies, the section might just be finished early.

Moving south, conditions worsened. Shankend viaduct with its fifteen arches was 'a large work' in greywacke and rubble, followed by Whitrope tunnel where there were severe problems. Both contracts were in the hands of the builder William Ritson. At Whitrope on a wet day in March, puddles and slurry covered 'the boggy, mossy and rotten ground'. Being on the line's summit, it was 'the coldest, the

most stormy and perhaps the most moist' of the locations. Only masons and hewers were busy – the navvies taking a holiday as with coats on, they could not work, and without them, they were wet through.

Poor nutrition led to men suffering from scurvy, a vitamin deficiency linked to lack of fresh vegetables and fruit – notwithstanding being close to districts where nourishing foods were plentiful. At Langburnshiel, a large sod hut was transformed into a 'hotel with beds' and licensed to sell alcohol, but in July 1860 it was attacked in yet another affray. Carts bringing provisions from Hawick were being waylaid and robbed.

The Whitrope tunnel was below the hill of Sandy Edge where five construction shafts had been driven into sandstone and rock of varying thickness, but 425 gallons of water per minute were gushing into the voids. Both access and wet pits for drainage under the track bed had to be hewn. Tunnelling there was thoroughly dangerous – only 8 yards could be cut in a week, though 'the work might be done in less time if accidents and casualties did not occur to delay it'. Shifts of 10 hours were the rule but the recommendation was that these should be cut to 8 hours. At the time of the inspection, there were 230 men on tunnel work but more masons were required to complete the brick lining. Ventilation, supplied by air boxes worked by fans attached to steam engines, was deficient, while breakdowns of machinery and protest strikes caused further interruptions. When complete, the tunnel – at 1,208yds

**Below left:** The plaque marking Whitrope Summit, 1,006ft (306.6m) above sea level.

**Below:** Whitrope siding signal box was a welcome sight for enginemen on the long hauls over the Waverley Route. (J L Stevenson)

Although Whitrope never had a station, the Waverley Route Heritage Association now has a visitor centre there.

Shankend viaduct is a 19 arch masterpiece, designed by the NBR engineer Charles Jopp, and formed from difficult greywacke rock.

The south entrance to the notorious mile-long tunnel at Whitrope on the Waverley Route to Carlisle.

The island platform at Riccarton Junction was on a curve and the station was modest but housed a range of facilities including a post office and refreshment rooms. (J L Stevenson)

(1,104m) —was the longest in Scotland, with a rising gradient of 1 in 90 going south.

Earth moving was being done on a grand scale – for example, the cutting at Ninestanerigg was 1,000 yd (914m) long and 65 ft(19.8m) deep, followed by an embankment 97 ft (29m) high. There was trouble with another deep cutting where 'the slope of ½ to 1 will not be nearly sufficient …and the loose rock, only supported by crumbling and rotten strata and stones, will fall down and cause heavy expense to the permanent way'. Although a massive embankment and large culvert at the Laidlehope burn were judged 'workmanlike', there were other daunting structures along the route and completion in the uplands was at least ten months away.

Small wonder that Ritson was minded to stop unless he was helped. He was given an advance of £2,000 by the NBR board with more to come, but two directors refused support. Their personal liabilities as guarantors of loans had become worryingly high, and there were more expenses for Bills in Parliament to meet. Even so, Hodgson found £3,000 to encourage the Border Counties Railway to proceed – this line would meet the NBR at Riccarton in remote terrain completely dependent on rail access. To speed the project, Ritson negotiated the hire of a locomotive from the NBR, for which he had to pay, and to avoid his quitting, from May 1861 he was allowed £1500 a month by the company. Track laying was now in view with chairs delivered to Gretna, and Baltic redwood sleepers imported via Fisherrow.

Just as on the E&HR, station completions – at Newcastleton, Barnes (later Stobs) and Shankend – were held back. Meantime, surfacemen's cottages would have to serve as stations. Platforms at Hawick station were made out of sleepers – these lightened the load on the Teviot viaduct and saved expense. Any woodwork was done at low cost and sidings were laid with discarded rails.

Further south in easier terrain, the contracts appeared more satisfactory. The inspection showed that both the Hermitage viaduct and the bridge over the Liddel were of good stone. With that river diverted, as its banks were 'not so firm', extra drainage was needed. An iron girder bridge had been placed over the Esk. The branches to Langholm and the Canonbie coal pits were advancing. The route then proceeded:

*'down to Longtown and Carlisle through fine, rich, level and open country, giving an idea of a full 5 per cent line'.*

– NBR Minutes of Directors 28 March 1861

To attain such a dividend from the Border Union Railway would prove impossible for the company. However, the construction news for the NBR directors was generally better here – some locations were 'ballasted, hedged and fenced' with station houses and other buildings under construction. It was even possible to travel on an engine about 7 miles to within sight of Carlisle. The line eventually had a succession of stations south from Steele Road, through Newcastleton and onwards over the 'debateable land' on the English-Scottish boundary to the Solway plain.

Nevertheless, it would take two years and ten months until the Border Union Railway could be opened throughout on 1 August 1862. Even in March that year, there was trouble, this time from labourers at the Dalston Burn near Newcastleton. Extra constables had to be sent to bring order – attributed to neglect by both the Excise and the police over the sale of unlicensed liquor. The Whitrope, Riccarton and Hermitage sections were also beset by further delays. Then the contractors for the Carlisle section went bankrupt and

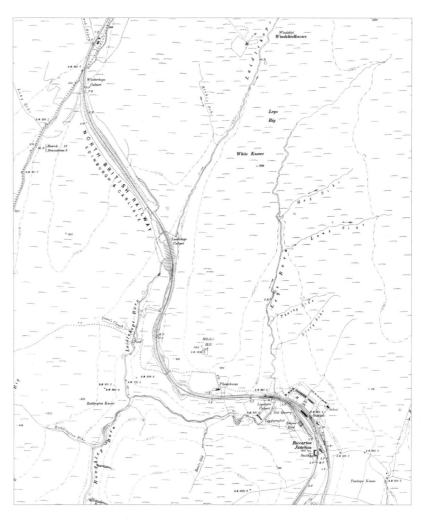

Charles Jopp, the NBR engineer, was instructed to use direct labour to complete the line. The Shankend viaduct and the Leaderfoot viaduct on the Berwickshire Railway are both monuments to his skills.

At a shareholders' meeting in March 1862, Hodgson gave a report on the Border Union Railway where expenditure had been 'much more formidable' than expected – circumstances he attributed to 'the influence of the seasons'. This was 'spin doctoring' of a high order. The estimate had been £500,000 but the figure by September

Riccarton Junction as shown on the Ordnance Survey 6 inch to the mile map of 1896 – a remote place over 800ft up reached by an exposed railway line. Note the Laidlehope burn with its culvert and major earthworks. (National Library of Scotland Map Room)

The opening day of the Border Counties Railway at Riccarton Junction on 1 July 1862, when the Border Union Railway also opened. (M Halbert Collection)

Journey's end for the NBR's Waverley Route was at Carlisle Canal depot where this tall signal box stood guard. (W S Sellar)

1861 was £835,955. Far from adverse weather, or the navvies and their drink problems, it was cut price contracts, poor management and lack of supervision of a challenging project that were at the root of the matter. The engineer in overall charge, J F Tone, a friend of Hodgson, would subsequently be judged lax in both attendance and effort.

In the circumstances, the NBR refused a request from the Hawick Poor House for a 'testimonial' to the governor and matron who had 'rendered service to sick comrades' – men employed on the Border Union project – and suggested that the contractors should be asked to contribute. However, if assistance could be given by the NBR without cost, it was a different matter, and so Hawick Total Abstainers were allowed the use of the old station for a meeting on New Year's Eve – Hogmanay festivities usually being noted for excessive consumption of alcohol.

By 1862 the lines at last reached Carlisle and the NBR quartered itself at Canal Street in that town. This might seem an odd name for a railway depot but a desire for improvements to the River Eden to assist navigation led to an Act in 1819 for a canal from Carlisle to the Solway Firth. Four years later the 11¼ mile (18km) route was navigable from a basin in the town to a harbour at Fisher's Cross. This was renamed 'Port Carlisle' and was suitable for the sea-going vessels of the time. By 1839 and the advent of the

Newcastle & Carlisle Railway, the canal was prospering but as other railways developed, canal trade ebbed away. In 1852, there were plans to convert the waterway to a railway and within two years tracks had been laid for the Port Carlisle Dock & Company's line. When the NBR approached Carlisle in 1862, it took over the old route.

As a harbour, Port Carlisle soon proved inadequate in comparison with Maryport on the Cumbrian coast, and in 1856 the railway was extended to Silloth where a new dock was built. To encourage trade, the old founding company then began to develop Silloth as a resort but it got into serious debt, only being rescued by a lease negotiated with the NBR. To that company, Silloth opened up prospects of trade by sea to both Liverpool and Ireland.

Silloth also offered a means of circumventing problems at Carlisle itself. Although the southern sections of the Border Union were fit to take traffic in September 1861, the NBR faced obstruction from the Caledonian Railway. For want of a set of points, there was no link between the NBR Port Carlisle branch and the old line of the Silloth company. This was single and the Board of Trade insisted on a double track. Only when this had been laid reluctantly by the Caledonian company were NBR trains able to access Carlisle Citadel station. The distance was just 1½ miles but the Caledonian charged for 4 miles – and the NBR made passengers pay by hiking up the fares. If the latter grumbled, they were told that it was the Caledonian's fault. The nastiness continued when the Caledonian would not allow NBR telegraph wires to go up on its track sides, or permit NBR pass holders to travel freely.

The Border Union Railway was brought into use in stages, the first 14 miles (22.5 km) from Carlisle to Scotsdyke being available for goods on 12 October 1861 and for passengers later that month. On 1 July 1862 the line was opened throughout from Hawick to Carlisle. As the new railway passed through territory that was the setting for several Scott novels, the NBR lost no time in advertising the line as 'The Waverley Route' and a special train from Edinburgh was run to launch it. At Carlisle, a luncheon was held in the carriage shed for some 700 guests. Hodgson

North British Railway had interests in Cumbria where its lines served Silloth docks – a view in LNER years. (Glen Collection)

was the centre of attention, praising the unprecedented expansion of the North British Railway, and even suggesting that it might soon be in the Highlands

On the same day, the Border Counties Railway, coming from Northumberland, also opened and its arrival made Riccarton a junction. The covetous Hodgson supplied it with funds that the NBR could ill afford, and he acquired it, thereby giving the NBR a better means of accessing Newcastle-upon-Tyne. The company had already bought land for a station there. Plashetts coal was now accessible and was forthwith promoted for Border mills and stipulated for use at NBR stations; however, it proved unsuitable for steam raising, being fit only for domestic purposes.

Earlier, the NBR directors had flirted with the Wansbeck Railway in Northumbria. This single track line of 26 miles (41.8 km) was authorised in 1859 to run from Reedsmouth to Morpeth on the East Coast main line of the North Eastern Railway. It was partially opened in 1862 but it took another three years to reach Reedsmouth by which time Hodgson had sucked it into the NBR system. However, its attractiveness had by then gone – it had been supplanted by the connection to Newcastle through Hexham.

Those who travelled over the Border Union Railway on its opening day would have seen abandoned work sites and rusting equipment en route to Carlisle. Ritson had pled to be allowed to remove machinery and plant but this was refused, Hodgson demanding that it be auctioned. Accordingly, in December 1862, a sale of contractor's equipment was advertised in 'The Railway Times'. It was a January 'roup' over three days in bleak locations at Whitrope and Shankend. Intending bidders were invited to join trains from Carlisle, Edinburgh and Newcastle stopping at the site, any purchasers being promised refreshments. The list of bargains was lengthy, from stationery steam engines, boilers, pumps and fans to earth barrows, carts, harness, blacksmiths' tools, rails and the navvy huts – 'a great variety of costly and useful articles'. The horses had been sold earlier for £400. There were over 350 wagons, large and small, including some curiosities such as 'fiddlestick' and 'pedestal' vehicles, the list giving an insight into railway contracting in the 1860s.

Coal mined at Plashetts in the Cheviot Hills was widely promoted by the North British Railway but proved unsuitable for steam raising. (R W Lynn)

Although the Border Union Railway had cost much more than estimated, Hodgson's expansive aims continued and tenders were issued for the Langholm, Peebles and Galashiels branches, and for the Berwickshire Railway. To encourage freight traffic at Hawick – and hopefully improve cash flow – goods rates were halved. Meanwhile the NBR was seeking penalty payments from the contractors on the Hawick and Hermitage sections, while further construction had yet to be done between Riddings and Riccarton Junctions.

The troubles were not over as the Gretna branch also suffered obstruction from the Caledonian company, test bores at Canonbie coalfield disappointed and the branch to Langholm took until April 1864 to open. The Byreburn viaduct, one of three giving access to the burgh, collapsed due to defective bricks being used in its construction and so access by rail was severed with inconvenience to the mills and distillery in the town. As a terminus, Langholm had a roofed station, giving carriages protection, plus an engine shed and turntable for the branch line engine.

Riccarton Junction, where the two Border lines met, became one of the oddest places on the British network. At 842ft (256.6m) up, 'in the middle of nowhere', it was

Riddings Junction was where the Langholm branch took off (left) to serve settlements along a route with tall viaducts. (J L Stevenson)

The regular branch train hauled by NBR No.22 is seen at Langholm station, which had a protective roof and engine shed but only a small staff. (R W Lynn Collection)

entirely dependent on the railway, the nearest habitation being at Nether and Over Riccarton and their mill, two miles away on a minor road from Jedburgh. At first, navvy huts were converted for accommodation, then a curved island platform, unique on the line, was built of timber to carry a simple station with refreshment rooms. A succession of railway requirements followed – a water tank, an engine shed, two signal boxes, a smithy, sidings, a coaling bank and a turntable (42ft at £290). Extra housing was constructed for employees and a substantial dwelling for the stationmaster. A gas works was installed to provide lighting and in 1877 a school and a shop were set up.

Emergency support for the isolated community came from Hawick where an engine was kept in steam to bring assistance if required. Initially on Sundays Riccarton residents worshipped in the engine shed until a train was run to take people to church in Hawick, or to Newcastleton. When the directors learned about 'misconduct' on such jaunts, five shilling fines were levied on the culprits. Perhaps the isolated location attracted less conventional employees.

The timetable for the Waverley Route showed four trains each way between Edinburgh and Carlisle. Described as express, fast, local and Parliamentary, the fast and express both took 3 hours 3 minutes for the 98½ miles (158.5km), the local and Parliamentary 4 hours 26

minutes. For passengers on the express or the fast, there were connections at Carlisle and those leaving Edinburgh at 9.45am could be in London (Euston) by 9.50pm. There were no through carriages. Two slow stopping trains ran to Carlisle on Sundays. Melrose people were soon complaining about the deterioration in train services there – upgrading to a main line meaning that expresses no longer stopped at Melrose – but the NBR, to its credit, did adjust the schedule.

By the time the Border Union Railway was complete, the North British Railway was facing serious trouble. The line had been planned as a major Anglo-Scottish trunk route but in reality it could never assume that role. From the beginning, the London & North Western and the Caledonian companies effectively blockaded the NBR at Carlisle, ensuring that 'unconsigned' freight arriving from the south was routed over the Caledonian. This made sense as there was a faster journey in prospect via Carstairs to Edinburgh, but the NBR lost what it believed should have been its business. The Waverley Route was not proving a commercial success, being condemned to function as a local line through the Borders and yielding only the revenue of a branch. It was even suggested that the southern portion should be abandoned or given over to any English company willing to take it on. The NBR considered giving up the issue of return tickets – two singles produced more revenue, a ruse that would increase cash flow. Moreover, reports showed that engines working hard on the Waverley Route were setting the moors and plantations on fire, leading to demands for compensation.

And calls for expenditure kept coming. In 1861, the condition of some of the original wooden bridges on the Edinburgh-Hawick line was such that three had to be replaced with iron structures. The contractor was James Tod & Sons of Edinburgh, a company dating from 1810, that by the 1860s was capable of supplying railways with a range of equipment, including signals for the Border Union. Scotland's iron industry was flourishing and the making of malleable iron came to the fore. Its manufacture required 'puddling', a dangerous and gruelling task involving stirring the molten metal in a furnace.

The sign board at Riddings Junction reminding passengers of the options on the branch line. (J L Stevenson)

Hawick station was a major facility on the Waverley Route giving support to the North British outpost at Riccarton Junction. (J L Stevenson Collection)

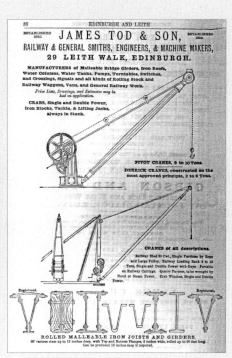

An advertisement for malleable iron goods supplied by James Tod & Son of Edinburgh, a company that replaced three bridges on the Edinburgh-Hawick line in 1861.

(Post Office Directory for Edinburgh & Leith 1868-69)

One of many bridges across the Gala Water that were originally wooden and later replaced with malleable iron structures; this hogsback design is a post-1880 structure.

ABBOTSFORD FROM THE TWEED.

Abbotsford, Sir Walter Scott's mansion on the banks of the River Tweed, was reached from a small station where a rowing boat took visitors to the estate. In 1867 Queen Victoria preferred to use her own carriage. (Glen Collection)

St Pancras station in London was the headquarters of the wealthy Midland Railway. The buildings in Gothic Revival style are now acclaimed. (Wikipedia)

a process that made the iron both flexible and strong. Puddlers were highly skilled and highly paid. (Major works, such as those of Gartsherrie and Summerlee at Coatbridge, were producing malleable iron on such a scale that the rapid expansion of railways, steam ships and construction of all kinds could be supported).

By the mid-1860s, the reorganisation of the Scottish railway companies was in the air. For some years, the NBR directorate had been pre-occupied with Bills for the company's likely amalgamation with the Edinburgh, Perth & Dundee Railway and, by an Act of 1862, it took over that company. The year 1865 saw numerous early railway companies coming together and five distinct entities emerged – the North British, the Caledonian, the Glasgow & South Western, the Highland and the Great North of Scotland. Crucially the NBR absorbed the prosperous Edinburgh & Glasgow. A new 'corporate identity' was badly needed, but finding the money for better uniforms was difficult. Railway companies were organisations that followed military patterns, but on the old NBR some grades

only got coats and some no garments at all. By contrast, the E&G had more generous practices that after the amalgamation were adopted by the NBR. Uniforms indicated status – frock coats and caps with gold braid being for stationmasters, waistcoats and moleskin trousers for lesser grades.

By 1865, the NBR was in Fife, in Glasgow and had reached Carlisle, but such expansion had come at a heavy price. In Hodgson's eagerness to gain territory for the NBR network, latterly he was prepared to accept the third-rate and to reduce spending wherever possible. The result was that locomotives, signalling, stations and track were in poor condition and requiring a great deal of money to be spent on them to achieve an efficient operation. The financial position of the company was deteriorating and at directors' meetings discussion of the accounts was regularly deferred.

Notwithstanding the generally respectable image of the NBR and its regular, if small, dividends, the company was facing a funding crisis. In May 1866, the failure of the Overend Gurney bank in London precipitated a widespread financial collapse, the British economy went into recession and railway stocks were badly affected. It soon emerged that the NBR's finances had long been in disarray – the practice had grown of massaging the accounts to conceal deficiencies, giving an impression of well doing to maintain the confidence of shareholders. To offer a modest return – thereby supporting the share price on the Stock Markets – interest on stock was being paid out of capital. When a new company secretary 'blew the whistle', the scandal broke. The damage to the reputation of the NBR was severe, and Hodgson and his fellow directors were forced to resign. A new board, committed to a policy of rigorous austerity, was appointed. A Committee of Investigation found that 'misrepresentation, deception and the deliberate falsification of the accounts', had been going on for years. Some argued that the directors should be imprisoned. This financial debacle was to haunt the NBR for decades as investors did not easily forget. In 1867, the company's debt was £1.8 million (estimated as £54 million in 2015).

Amid the gloom, a Royal Visit was a diversion. On 21 August 1867, Queen Victoria came over the Waverley Route from Carlisle, the train slowing down at a thronged Hawick station on the way to Kelso. There the NBR directors allowed a sum 'not exceeding £25' to be spent on station decorations and an ornamental shelter. Special trains were run to Kelso from Galashiels and Edinburgh 'at moderate fares'. The following day, the Queen visited Melrose and Abbotsford, both being places of pilgrimage in Scott's memory. She commented on the crowds at the roadsides and found Galashiels "very prettily situated, & a flourishing manufacturing town, where tweeds and shawls are made". The men known as "the braw lads" were supposed to be "rather uproarious".

Meanwhile the wealthy Midland Railway had a project to construct an independent line of its own through the desolate Northern Pennines to Carlisle. The Midland had come late to main line operations and it found such companies as the London & North Western opposed to it. Likewise, the NBR viewed the Caledonian Railway, the LNWR's West Coast partner, as hostile – hence the Midland and the NBR could comfortably join forces for their own purposes. Already in 1873, the Midland had leased premises in Edinburgh's Princes Street from the NBR, and the following year was taking an interest in a proposal for a Forth Bridge.

The Midland Railway's headquarters were at Derby, from where it focussed on the East Midlands and North Yorkshire. Through joint running powers on shared lines, it had links to York, Manchester, Birmingham and Bristol. Its London base was at St Pancras. The Midland had become the third largest railway company in Britain and the biggest coal haulier – it was therefore an influential and prosperous partner for the NBR to have.

In 1865 the Midland aimed to secure parliamentary approval for a Bill for its own route from Leeds to Carlisle. At the time, its relationship with the LNWR was strained, although this did improve and the MR had second thoughts – even trying to abandon the Bill for its Settle & Carlisle Railway (a move that the NBR actually opposed), but it was too late. So the Midland was forced into building this arduous and expensive line, the highest in England, reaching a summit of 1,169ft (356m) at Ais Gill. Construction commenced in 1869 and continued for seven years until the 72 mile long route was complete. Although it followed natural pathways, such as the Eden valley, no fewer than 20 viaducts and 14 tunnels were required. It would be the last main line in Britain to be constructed by hand labour and it took a dreadful toll in accidents and outbreaks of disease. The Midland engineers tried to design the line for high speed running but it was to prove slower than either the East or West Coast routes – nowadays being acclaimed as 'scenic' rather than fast.

Meanwhile, the NBR's Border Union was performing poorly and a letter from the South of Scotland Chamber of Commerce lodged complaints. The reply from the NBR management was conciliatory, 'The Directors hope shortly on the Opening of the Settle & Carlisle line to make improved arrangements and that, in the meantime, the delays are attributable to the irregularities of trains from the south'.

In 1874 the problem was tackled by the NBR with a train from Hawick to Edinburgh running in front of the express from Carlisle, the timetable warning that NBR trains would no longer wait the arrival of 'much delayed' services from the south.

Through the 1870s, the NBR was in a state of continuing austerity arising from the financial debacle of 1866. Capital expenditure was viewed as 'pernicious', and receipts lagged behind working expenses. For any new or replacement works, the directors instructed that the lowest tender should be accepted. In August 1871, it was proposed to divert the Gala Water at Fountainhall, where it encroached on the station, and also at Bowland. But would lowest tenders ensure 'proper work'? Nevertheless, the river was re-located to its present course. In January 1873 a collapse at Borthwick Bank was so serious that more land was required to widen the base. The NBR directors disliked spending money, and only after the intervention of the Procurator-Fiscal of Selkirk was the timber bridge over the Tweed below the Ettrick Water on the Selkirk branch reconstructed with six piers and iron girders.

In 1875, possibly with a view to the Midland Railway's intention to run over the Waverley Route and use longer rolling stock, Bowshank tunnel was widened 'by about five feet in the centre'. Tunnelling was not an exact science and Bowshank was irregular in form with 'the rails being too close to the wall, and the roofs of the carriages nearly grazing the brick arch'. About 50 men were employed on 'delicate and difficult engineering work' to remove half the arch and to excavate the rock with 'crowbar and pick'. A new half-arch was then built on a wider base. Meanwhile, trains continued to run on a single line 'with little interruption and no accident'- a limited installation of block signalling being in use.

Generally, savings were made wherever possible – when permanent way staff asked for topcoats and leggings, this was refused and the NBR's police were denied improved uniforms. Scrap, whether old engines or old iron, was sold at the best price obtainable. The Locomotive Superintendent had to be adept at rebuilding engines from 'write offs'. So restrictive were the limits on expenditure that there were problems with the overheating of axles on vehicles due to insufficient grease being available. Indeed, the Board of Trade was most concerned about the company's practices, notably its reluctance to install the block system with interlocking for signals and points throughout the NBR network. By 1874, only some 25 per cent of its system was thus protected. The NBR was not alone in having deficiencies. A Royal Commission on Railway Accidents reported that railway workers were a third more likely to suffer injury compared with other industrial workers. Railways were very dangerous places on which to be employed.

In this phase, hard bargains were driven over any purchases. With a requirement for 2,000 tons of locomotive coal per month (at 5s 1d per ton, about 25p), the NBR wisely shopped around for supplies, and for every item it used. Nevertheless, some modest advances in wages and salaries for key staff were permitted – probably to discourage men from leaving for other employment. Unusual

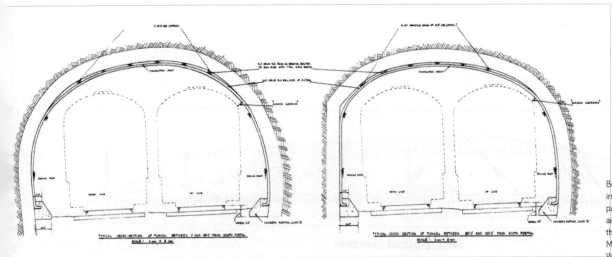

Bowshank tunnel was irregular in shape and was partially widened in 1875 to accommodate the carriages that would be used by the Midland Railway on the Waverley Route. (Network Rail)

A luggage label from the Midland Railway issued to ensure that the consignment went along the Waverley Route. (Glen Collection)

A Midland Railway advertisement for the Waverley Route shows a 'Scotch Comic', hardly the image for the line that the North British tried to project. (Glen Collection)

generosity was shown in February 1875 when farmers at Falahill were given passes for a year in recognition of their help in digging out snow-blocked trains.

The adverse views of some shareholders about the Border Union Railway softened somewhat when the wealthy Midland Railway at last completed its Settle & Carlisle route from Leeds to the Border city in 1876. Goods trains from Carlisle could now run north on the NBR line and the hope was that Midland traffic would feed into the NBR services to Edinburgh and the Glasgow & South Western Railway's line to Glasgow, thereby challenging the Caledonian's grip on traffic heading along the West Coast main line. Through services for passengers from London to Edinburgh via the Waverley Route began on 1 May 1876. For its part, the NBR advertised 'eight day Cheap Special Excursions from Edinburgh Waverley Station to St Pancras Station, London, by the Waverley and New Midland Route'.

The Midland Railway had come late to main line operations and its trains were slower than those of the East Coast or West Coast companies. It compensated for this by offering passengers greater comfort, and thereby stole a march on its competitors. In 1872 it put third class passengers into its second class carriages – and abolished the latter class. Its 'third class' stock thus became *upholstered* – leading to the accusation that it 'pampered the working class'. This put the NBR directors in a quandary over 'cushioning' in their vehicles and the extra expense that this would incur.

The Midland also won custom by reducing first class fares to the old second class level. It introduced bogie coaches (these had two sets of four wheels per carriage). Of a superior design to anything the NBR could offer, they were turned out in crimson lake and the ' Midland Scotch Joint Stock', was said to 'run like a dream', giving a much smoother passage over the Waverley Route than the NBR's six-wheelers. Nevertheless, the NBR had to provide the locomotives to take the trains to and from Carlisle and the Midland vehicles were heavy. The NBR engines were simply inadequate for the task.

The Midland Railway had other ambitions too. Pullman cars were an American innovation and in 1870 the enterprising George Pullman had come to Britain. He arranged to supply the Midland with his cars in kit form, thus introducing luxury travel on its services. These were a sensation – trains of Pullman cars would come to symbolise *grand luxe* on railways and a trial run soon took place over the Waverley Route. A dissatisfied passenger at Newtown St Boswells asked the NBR when an 'Up Pullman Train' might stop at his station.

By the summer of 1877, the Midland Railway wished an extra through passenger train service between St Pancras and Edinburgh, but the NBR committee 'could not see their way to accede to this request at present' – motive power was lacking. Then the Midland proposed to run an additional night express to which the NBR could only give 'provisional agreement'. The company was finding it difficult to keep up with its eager partner. Nevertheless, a payment of £1,200 a year for working through traffic for the Midland at Carlisle, was a welcome addition to income.

On local trains, it was a different story. There were complaints not only about NBR time-keeping but criticism of its comfortless 'shaking' carriages. New orders were needed but the NBR already owed £28,000 (estimated at £840,000 in 2015) to its Manchester supplier. There were many other deficiencies, one being the absence of footbridges at stations – even busy places such as Hawick had only 'board crossings' at track level, leading to accidents. Any footbridges sanctioned were basic – just wooden stairs with a handrail and wire fencing. When a footbridge over the line at Buckholmside at Galashiels fell down, the directors questioned their obligation to replace it. Nevertheless, safety at level crossings in that town was improved by having electric bells installed between the signal boxes and the crossings. Only in 1877 was a long lattice girder bridge ('the cheapest for iron and mason work') constructed over the lines at the station to carry the turnpike road across the railway. Another improvement was the supply of clocks to level crossing keepers so that they might know when trains were expected.

With strict finances, revenue protection came to the fore – tickets were being checked at 'other than the usual ticket examining stations'. To assist staff, from January 1874 continuous footboards on the outside of carriages were adopted throughout the NBR Non-payment of fares was met with a fine, and in some instances by imprisonment. Thefts

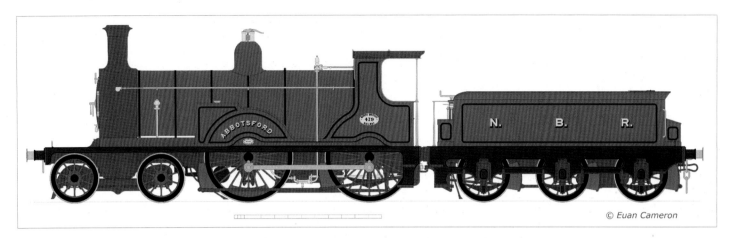

© Euan Cameron

especially from goods yards, were frequent and so in addition to the NBR's own railway police, 'secret detectives' were suggested. These were in fact porters and guards urged to use extra vigilance. Such were the frauds at Eskbank that the entire staff was sacked, and there was much concern over 'outstandings' at other stations arising from miscalculations, or possibly poor bookkeeping. At Hawick, the stationmaster was demoted – by being moved to a smaller place.

A positive step for passengers was the arranging of leases for refreshment rooms at Melrose, Kelso, St Boswells and Galashiels stations. In 1861 a sheriff travelling regularly from the Borders to Edinburgh, had written to the NBR directors suggesting that train toilets would be a good idea. However, before carriages had corridors, there were no toilets on trains – unless in private saloons or special vehicles. Passengers had to wait for a stop at a station where facilities were available – these were the ones with refreshment rooms and 'waiting rooms' for different classes – usually at junctions where trains were changed. (The ornamental cast iron urinal from Melrose station is now in the care of the Severn Valley Railway).

By 1875, the NBR, under prudent management, was beginning to see some relative prosperity and an exacting locomotive superintendent was appointed. This was Dugald Drummond, a dour but determined Scot, who had considerable experience in mechanical engineering and railway operations. He had worked with William Stroudley on the Brighton line where fast running was the norm and he must have found the NBR depressing – it had only eight express locomotives in its stock. He identified a pressing need for engines fit to work the new Waverley-Carlisle expresses over the curving and steep grades of that route. The NBR's old 4-4-0s were performing poorly with the heavy coaching stock off the Midland. There was thus an urgent need for new locomotives and Drummond did not disappoint:

*'The engines he designed not only hauled the new heavy trains at higher speeds over the most difficult main line in the country but established their designer as a locomotive engineer of the first rank'.* – Locomotives of the North British Railway, 1846-1882, The Stephenson Locomotive Society

The Drummond class of 4-4-0s were robust but neat and won much praise. According to O.S. Nock the railway author, 'no locomotive work at that period could better that of the NBR over the severe gradients of the Waverley route'.

Typically, the passenger locomotives carried the names of places they served – *Abbotsford, Eskbank, Galashiels, Hawick, Melrose, Newcastleton, St Boswells,* and even *Carlisle,* appeared. For places served by the company, it was good

publicity – nevertheless, the names confused some passengers who thought they were train destinations. The practice continued with tank engines for local services. Drummond also designed many goods engines for the company's substantial mineral traffic; these were 0-6-0 locomotives built both by the NBR at its Cowlairs works and by the Glasgow builders Dübs and Neilson.

In the interests of safety, Drummond held brake trials in December 1876 on the Edinburgh-Glasgow route. This tested rival systems – Westinghouse and Smith's Vacuum apparatus. Trains of eight carriages with a brake van at each end were prepared, and Westinghouse emerged the winner. This involved attaching an air pump to locomotives and its rhythmic sound, from engines stopped at stations, came to characterise NBR trains. However, the Midland Railway opted for the vacuum brake leading to the 'dual fitting' of joint stock for the Waverley Route.

With Midland expresses now stopping to take water, Riccarton Junction was not forgotten. More company houses were built for workmen's families for which they had to pay an annual rent. The Education (Scotland) Act of 1872 required new primary schools to be erected. So the NBR sold land to the School Board of Castleton for a school and schoolmaster's house. There were few instances of NBR generosity, but a small contribution was given to a 'Free Library' at the junction. In 1876 there was heavy snow in late December when eight goods trains became stranded on the Waverley Route and drifts of fifteen feet were reported, but the NBR had only one large snow plough. On such occasions, the men at Riccarton were on snow clearing duties round the clock.

By 1878 there were two London expresses out and back from Edinburgh via Carlisle each weekday taking 10 hours

Dugald Drummond's 'Abbotsford' class of neat 4-4-0 locomotives of 1878 performed impressively on the sinuous and steep Waverley Route. (Euan Cameron)

For branch lines, Drummond borrowed ideas from Stroudley's 'Terrier' 0-6-0 tank engines, naming them after the branches on which they were to run. (Euan Cameron)

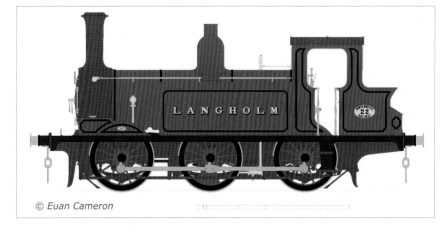

© Euan Cameron

45 minutes for the journey to St Pancras. The line wound its way through the 'Scott country' famed in song and legend. Slow though the journey was, the Borders countryside, with woods and farmland set among hills and rivers, appealed to city dwellers, especially those from England's industrial areas. The views were not dramatic, but the scenery had become invested with a special quality through the writings of Sir Walter Scott. The readers of the historical novels flocked to the Borders on the NBR's trains to see the places for themselves and to experience their ambience.

Before the Edinburgh & Hawick Railway opened, flowing water had been driving a fifth of the spindles in the Border woollen mills, and many more were hand operated. The North British Railway not only transported regular supplies of coal from the Lothians and other mineral fields, it also brought in bales of quality wool from England, from Australia and from remote Kashmir. Such fibres gave fine yarns for knitwear and cloth of outstanding quality. The railway's presence, more than any other factor, helps to explain the sheer density of the textile and woollen industry that arose in the Border towns of Galashiels, Hawick and Selkirk.

In January 1879 the renewal of bridges 'as may be required' in the NBR's South Section, was announced. At Torwoodlee, the two span wooden bridge was rebuilt with malleable iron beams and new piers, costing £1,495. The bitter winter had caused severe ice blockage at the wooden bridge at Bowshank – its twelve 10ft spans were 'low and heavy' and the Gala Water burst its banks. The present malleable iron skewed span with 'massive box-latticed girders, resting on stone abutments', and costing £2,699, came from Skerne Iron Works in Darlington. The under bridges at Watherston and Galabank were also replaced by Skerne. It would take several years before the dozen other wooden bridges over the Gala Water disappeared. Ever sparing, the NBR always took the lowest tender.

As if to mark how far the NBR had come since the financial debacle of the mid-1860s, by 1877 it could boast an engineering wonder – the new rail viaduct linking Fife with Dundee. It stretched for 2 miles across the open waters of the Firth of Tay and that summer was traversed by Queen Victoria with due ceremony. In a winter storm of 28 December 1879, the structure collapsed taking a passenger train with it.

It was a national catastrophe and raised questions about the strength of materials, meteorology, wind loading and about engineering. The NBR directors almost immediately determined to construct a replacement viaduct that continues in use, but preliminary work on a Forth Bridge was stopped. However, from then on, there were those who would not cross the Firth of Tay on a NBR train under any circumstances, preferring 'the long way round' by Perth. There were searching enquiries and recommendations, the Board of Trade warning the NBR directors that they would be held responsible for the safety of all structures on their network. The long slog to rebuild confidence in the company had to begin once more.

**Top left:** Riccarton Junction in its final form, a railway outpost without a road link, 15 miles from Hawick, viewed in wintry conditions in 1963. (W S Sellar)

**Centre left:** Although steam power had become widespread, water from the Gala and other streams was essential for processing in the Borders woollen industry – flows being controlled by 'cauls' or weirs, and by sluices.

**Left:** The North British Railway transformed the Borders textile industry with its regular coal trains bringing fuel to supply steam power – here in Galash

# Expansion and Conflict

By the 1880s, the Border towns had been transformed by the railways and had won a name for their textiles. Galashiels had twenty mills and factories, mainly on the south side of the Gala Water, from Buckholm in the west to Netherdale in the east. The town bristled with chimney stalks putting smoke into the atmosphere and adding to the misery of winter fogs in the valley. It was now coal dependent for its industry, and for its gas works lighting homes, offices, mills and streets. A variety of products were made, including tweeds, tartans, and shawls, but fashion could prove fickle and output had to change with tastes. In 1883 the Galashiels Manufacturers' Corporation set up classes in textile production to improve skills and this soon evolved into a technical school. In addition to the mills, there were dye works, a skinnery, iron and brass foundries and engineering workshops making or repairing machinery. The town had a growing service sector with banks, insurance agencies, hotels and inns.

Although steam boilers now powered the mills, supplies of soft water were essential for processing wool, and so the cauls and mill leads on the Gala Water were maintained. This river was described as 'less powerful than the Tweed but more mischievous' – efforts were made to restrain its flow with bulwarks, and by straightening and deepening the channel. Even so, when torrential rain or snowmelt caused floods, it could inundate the lower parts of the town and cause much damage to property.

Where once open fields with tenter frames for drying and stretching blankets and rugs had lined the lower slopes, housing for the workforce had been built. Evidence of prosperity was seen in the villas and mansions of the mill owners on higher ground southeast of the town centre. Wool brokers became wealthy, trading regularly in London with contacts in Australia and New Zealand. The town had grown greatly – from a village in the 1840s to a town of 17,000 people by the 1880s – but was described in gazetteers as 'irregular' and 'straggling',

much of it being squeezed into the narrow valley.

Selkirk, on the right bank of the Ettrick Water, was once associated with 'souters' or shoemakers. After its branch line opened in 1856, the burgh had a similar development to Galashiels. With plentiful supplies of coal, its mills soon increased in number, expanding its output of cloth and tweed as its reputation for quality products grew. A speciality was 'shepherd tartan', in a small black and white check, favoured by Sir Walter Scott. By 1881 Selkirk's population had trebled to 6,090.

Hawick's textile industry began with the spinning of woollen yarn and knitting in the homes of the local farming community. In 1771 knitting frames were introduced and by the 1840s the town led in this craft, stockings being the main output. However, water power from the Rivers Teviot and Slitrig was irregular and another Borders' transformation came after 1849 when coal could be conveyed in wagon loads on the railway. A profusion of knitted woollen goods, from outer garments to underwear, was soon produced by ten mills and thirteen hosiery manufacturers. The labels of Hawick companies – Ballantine, Peter Scott and Pringle among others – would become well known and most products were sent to customers in goods vans or as parcels, making a lucrative trade for the railway. The burgh was also a service and social centre with a population approaching 12,000.

The NBR itself had become a significant employer in the Borders. A station, such as Galashiels, built in 1848, occupied a substantial area near the town centre, and being its stationmaster or 'station agent' was a position of some prestige. It now had three platforms with offices, refreshment and waiting rooms where clerks for both the passenger and goods business, and porters were on hand. Signalmen manned the boxes controlling the station and the extensive goods yard where a foreman and shunters worked. In addition, there were stables and warehouses. Every mill by the line had a siding supplied from the coal

**Far left:** Supplies of soft water from the Gala were drawn off for the textile industry; the flow being controlled by sluices that survive. These also assist flood control.

**Left:** Mills soon covered the valley floor out by Buckholmside in Galashiels where the old buildings have now found other uses.

Selkirk had a similar development to Galashiels to which its mills were closely tied. Coal brought by the railway allowed these to prosper. By the 1900s, the station had staff for both the passenger and goods traffic on the branch.
(R W Lynn Collection)

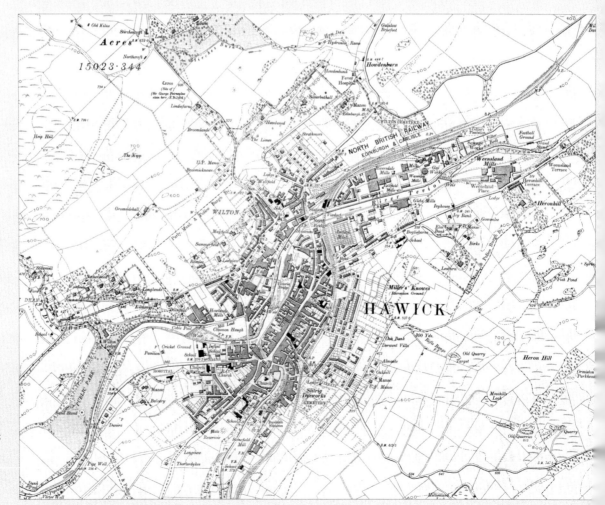

By the 1890s, the extent of railway installations in Hawick is shown in this excerpt from the Ordnance Survey 6-inch map of 1897; the viaduct over the River Teviot no longer exists and the auction mart for livestock has gone. (National Library of Scotland Map Room)

yards, while domestic fuel for grates and ranges was distributed in the town by cart.

Hawick was the dominant railway centre in the Borders, not only with its busy station and goods yards, but also having facilities for servicing locomotives. From the early days of the line, 'running repairs' could be carried out. Its engines of various classes covered a range of duties – double-heading on heavy trains, or assisting in banking up to Whitrope. Some would haul local services or special excursions. The 'yard pilot' shunted sidings round the clock. 'Pick up goods' trains were assignments for larger locomotives – dropping off or collecting freight vehicles at sidings on the Waverley Route, and spending all day on the task. Hawick's carriage and wagon examiners checked vehicles for hot axle boxes and other defects, permanent way men maintained the tracks, while specialist staff oversaw signal and telegraph equipment. Altogether, the NBR is reckoned to have had over 50 employees at Hawick in the 1890s.

The railways transformed many aspects of Borders farming. On the rolling hills, Blackface sheep had been largely replaced by thick-fleeced Cheviots supplying better quality wool. The livestock trade flourished as never before. For decades, Market Streets were where animals were penned or tethered for sale. After haggling over prices, bargains were settled with a handshake. After 1846 the trade benefited from the repeal of the Auction Tax that had levied one shilling in the pound on sales of moveable goods, including animals, and was viewed as 'iniquitous'. The auction method soon began whereby bids were 'cried' in open trading round an auction ring, the sales being conducted by an auctioneer. The firms of Oliver in Hawick and John Swan at St Boswells came to the fore as their businesses grew beside the NBR's tracks.

Once rail transport was available, the days of droving over long distances, with its many risks, were numbered. Trade moved to the new sidings and marts close to stations. Advertisements for property leases or farm sales emphasised the attraction of sites 'well served by the railway' and enhanced their value. Any driving of animals was now only a few miles – from farm to market or back – any further and the railway company had special vehicles for the purpose. Through the Border Union and the Border Counties lines, livestock from the Borders or North of England could be traded at Hawick, or sent to Wooler, Newcastle or Carlisle – wherever there was a price advantage.

By 1873, so expansive was business at Hawick that the NBR was looking for 5 acres to enlarge its yards, and it hoped for an increased water supply too. The Duke of Buccleuch, a noted benefactor to the town, was prepared to sell three acres for £576 and the NBR contributed £100 towards an improved road to the station. With unprecedented concentrations of livestock in transit, or in yards around its auction mart, Hawick could be like the 'Wild West' at times. Having a throughput of 25,000 sheep at the autumn lamb sales, animal welfare and the control of diseases became issues. The NBR was slow to respond. The failure to disinfect cattle wagons and pens at Kelso and at St Boswells led to the company being summoned in 1880 under 'The Contagious Diseases and Animals Act', and fined £5 plus £3 3s expenses. The method used involved lime wash, making treated vehicles white and the 'unclean' easy to detect.

By the 1880s there was greater awareness of what other railways were doing in terms of facilities for passengers and housing for employees. Passengers at Fushiebridge asked for

a shelter on the platform and a 'shed' was provided at £50. At Hardengreen, 'company servants' lodged a petition for housing, and additional cottages were authorised at Tynehead at £150. Surfacemen were often poorly served and housing at Langholm became an issue – the NBR was using premises for a local squad that were judged 'uninhabitable' and should be pulled down.

Passenger satisfaction with the NBR was generally disappointing. It was judged a poor provider, with charges too high, train times inconvenient, and its services slow, while requests for cheaper fares were fobbed off. 'Mixed trains' on some local services had old wagons coupled ahead of the carriages, some of the latter being described as 'hen coops on wheels'. Although some new rolling stock had been built – a new family carriage and a Post Office Sorting Van, for example – renewal of carriages was becoming an imperative. In 1882 there was a recommendation that 560 vehicles be replaced but only 'at the same rate as the last 4 years', a programme that would take no less than 6½ years to complete.

In spite of the NBR's shortcomings, the railway gave Borderers the opportunity for summer excursions and these were eagerly supported. Day trips to Edinburgh, or to the Clyde Coast for sails on NBR steamers, were attractive. Loch Lomond was a favourite destination – and was the venue for the NBR directors' annual excursion. All manner of societies organised such outings, from local trades and

*Hawick not only had a busy station (left centre) but also had extensive sidings and servicing facilities for the maintenance of locomotives and rolling stock. (J L Stevenson)*

*There was a peak of activity in Hawick goods yard at the autumn lamb sales. Here sheep are being put on rail trucks, disinfected with white lime wash, in 1896. (History of Andrew Oliver & Son Ltd, Hawick)*

temperance organisations to Sunday schools and church groups. Mill companies chartered trains to take their employees on excursions, and going to Silloth, now a resort at the seaside, was especially popular. In 1886, the International Exhibition of Industry, Science and Art, held in Edinburgh, drew tens of thousands of visitors and the NBR had a new 4-4-0 locomotive of its 592 class on display.

The NBR had a close relationship with Masonic Lodges and many railwaymen were staunch supporters. The directors and officers of the company were often Masons, some holding senior positions in that organisation. Masons were treated favourably when travelling to ceremonies 'at half the usual fare'. Similar consideration was given to charitable organisations, such as the Good Templars, a popular American group, or to the Foresters, another friendly society. The NBR even set up its own 'Workers Friendly Society'.

At Christmas 1885 came a special offer over the Waverley Route – Thomas Cook, the travel agent active in Edinburgh since the 1850s, had arranged five-day excursions with the NBR and the Midland to English towns such as Bolton, Bradford and Sheffield, plus the cities of Liverpool and Manchester, tickets for the latter two being £1 in First Class and 10 shillings (50p) in Third. (By 1887 Bradshaw noted two overnight trains with Pullman sleeping cars for first class only – hence the 'Sleeper' was known as 'The Pullman' in the Borders).

With the scattered Border towns now rail connected, trains could also carry crowds of supporters to sporting events. By the 1870s, rugby football clubs were emerging. The game, perceived as 'manly', relieved the routine of factory, mill or farm, and was soon based on local loyalties. Its Border origins may go back to the annual hand ba' games that were played in towns and villages where two 'ends' would take different sides. Such games continue at Duns, Hawick and Jedburgh each year. Another influence may have came from mill journeymen from Yorkshire who installed machinery in Borders' mills and had interests in 'Rugby League'.

Several rugby football clubs were set up in the 1870s – Hawick (1873), Gala (1875), Kelso (1876) and Melrose (1877), being among the oldest clubs in the world. In 1883 the first 'Sevens' tournament was held at Melrose. Thanks to the railway and its 'specials', hundreds of fans could travel by train to games 'home and away' and to internationals in Edinburgh. By 1901 a Border League was established and Borderers have made a unique contribution to the Scottish game. By comparison, association football emerged slowly with Gala Fairydean and Gala Rovers appearing in 1903 (but now amalgamated).

**Top:** Thanks to the railway, Newton St Boswells, with two auction marts, became a major centre of the livestock trade. These are the premises of John Swan & Company. (The Gazetteer for Scotland)
**Above centre:** The forgotten station at Fushiebridge, opened in 1847, where a shed was built for passengers. The station closed on 4 October 1943. (R W Lynn)
**Above:** The Midland Railway introduced Pullman cars to Britain in the 1870s. Here an early Pullman sleeping car for first class passengers only, as used on the Waverley Route, is seen in St Pancras station. (R C Riley)
**Right:** Melrose Rugby Football Club invented the 'Seven-a-Side' game in 1883 and this shows the first 'Sevens' team. The railway, carrying crowds of supporters to matches, helped to popularise rugby in the Borders. (Melrose RFC)

Holidays for employees in factory or mill might be only one week a year – and without pay. Favourite days to choose were at the Common Ridings in summer where traditionally the boundaries of a town's lands were inspected on horseback and its history celebrated. The records of Hawicks's Callants, of Selkirk's 'Birleymen' (burgh law men), and of Lauder's Common Riding are at least 400 years old. Such gatherings cemented local identities – the railways helping to popularise the events by making them more accessible than ever before.

The defence of the realm came to the attention of the NBR when the company was reminded by the War Office that cattle trucks had to be big enough to take horses in an emergency. After the Crimean War (1853-6), the Lord-Lieutenants of the counties were asked to form Volunteer Rifle Corps. Civilian part-timers were soon organised on regimental lines and Borderers participated with enthusiasm. Volunteers in uniform could travel on return trips 'at the single fare' In August 1881 there was a Royal Review in Edinburgh when volunteers from all over Britain came by special trains, including some over the Waverley Route. Owing to heavy downpours of rain, it became known as the 'Wet Review'.

Stations had become places of popular resort, not only for people travelling but also for those keeping an eye on the comings and goings of rural society. Some came to collect a daily paper from a stall on the platforms. This activity emphasised the railway's key role in the distribution of newspapers and magazines nationwide. There was also the telegraph – for railway use only, or jointly for the public if paid – giving stations extra significance. Every station had its goods yard with a siding, shed and crane. Here coal wagons, cattle trucks and vans would stand beside a loading bank where horse-drawn carts waited. Lime, manure, and agricultural equipment could be collected there, and products from farms and estates, such as grain, potatoes, timber and livestock, despatched. It was freight that made

most money for the NBR.

Though many NBR stations were basic and mundane, from the 1870s enamel signs began to appear. These were durable compared with paper advertisements, brightened walls and fences and raised income for railway companies. Such signs took products from relative obscurity to being household names. Many related to cleaning (Lux Flakes and Vim), or to being clean (Sunlight Soap and Jeyes Fluid);others were for foods and beverages (McVitties's Biscuits or Melrose's Tea), while health products were not overlooked (Virol or Andrew's Liver Salts). Such signs are now much valued as 'collectables'.

Regardless of temperance opinions, the NBR was willing to advertise alcohol, even although the company had its own Temperance Society and intoxication on railway duty usually brought dismissal. Advertisements also promoted cigarettes and tobacco, as from 1868 smoking was permitted on trains and there were compartments for smokers. Weighing machines, or those dispensing 'sweetmeats' for 'a penny in the slot', were also acceptable – these produced rent – but directors were less sure about 'Mutascope' amusements, possibly with 'what the butler saw' contents.

Although more attention was being paid to safety issues, trade unions such as the Amalgamated Society of Railway Servants, were abhorrent to railway companies. Strikes took place in the NBR's works in support of weeks shorter than 54 hours, accidents being ascribed to the long days

**Above:** This Midlands Railway advertisement shows its many connections. After the Forth Bridge opened in 1890, Aberdeen could also be reached via the North British Railway and the Waverley Route – hence the reference to 'Cock o' the North'. (Glen Collection)

Stations were places of popular resort with stalls for newspapers, telegraph facilities, and 'penny in the slot' machines in addition to tickets and goods offices. This busy scene is at St Boswells. (J L Stevenson Collection)

'Penny in the slot' machines were attractions at stations and earned rent for railway companies. This example printed nameplates.
(Beamish Museum)

worked. In response, the mean-minded company, putting shareholders first, cut a shilling off weekly wages. By 1882, the locomotive department men were asking for a 9 hour day, as it had become clear that some employees were spending as much as 18 hours on engine footplates. Accidents, often in excess of a hundred each year, were noted in the NBR Minute Books. When the School Board of Hawick requested higher parapets on an overbridge leading to a school, it had to pay for the work to be done – to the satisfaction of the company's engineer.

There were prolonged and bitter winters in the early 1880s when reports noted that the Ettrick was frozen at Abbotsford. Floods were a recurring theme leading to the continued renewal of bridges on the Gala Water. Offers came this time from Oliver & Arrol for replacements at Whitemyre for £1,080 and at Kilnknowe for £1,442. The following spring, the Gala was in destructive mode again and the NBR was asked to compensate for damaged property at Whitelee and other sites. Had the company been neglecting culverts and drainage? The railway's stables at Galashiels were washed away and a replacement cost £95. In 1881 P&W McLellan of Glasgow offered 'to supply, deliver and erect the malleable iron girders for the renewal

After damaging floods in 1881, the Whin Water bridge was replaced by this lattice girder structure from P&W MacLellan of Glasgow.
(G Rudman)

of the bridge over the Whin Water to the north of Galashiels' for the sum of £1,470 and this was accepted. Somervail & Company from Dalmuir works, Glasgow, installed a new low bridge for the school access at Bowland.

Despite the limits on spending money, in December 1880 a plan for proposed improvements at Riccarton Junction at a cost of about £2,000 was discussed. This mainly related to housing for the growing number of employees there and in 1882, two extra 'double houses' were built for £900. Riccarton's isolated location made it essential to have teams there for the effective operation and maintenance of the Waverley Route, and for snow clearance. Rent had to be paid to the NBR for houses.

In January 1891 adverse weather again took its toll on lines in the Borders when embankments collapsed and an abutment on a bridge near Whitrope gave way, making the 'Up Line' on the Waverley Route unsafe for traffic. And there was always that warning from the Railway Inspectorate to heed – the directors would be held responsible for the safety of structures on the company's lines. Accordingly, the Engineer-in-Chief was ordered to give 'constant attention to the Bridges'.

On 10 September 1891, the NBR directors received a letter from the Board of Trade about the renewal of iron bridges – cast iron was brittle and unreliable, but malleable iron was acceptable. Eleven days later 'the exceptionally heavy rainfall' had the General Manager reporting damage to bridges at Torwoodlee, Bowland (Whin Bridge), the viaduct on the Esk valley line, plus bridges on the Galashiels & Peebles and the Penicuik branches. A carved stone at the north entry to Bowshank tunnel shows the height the water reached on 19 September when flooding probably washed ballast out of the tunnel. The Engineer-in-Chief was now asked to report 'what should be done with a view to the protection of the line and the reconstruction of the bridges throughout the Gala Water District'. Reporting on 15 October, he was ordered to carry out the works, including the purchase of whatever land was required, charging two-thirds to revenue and one-third to capital. The vulnerability of this portion of the Waverley Route was again all too apparent.

Throughout the 1890s, the NBR made some effort to improve its railway properties – adding wash houses and coal stores to dwellings, and water closets to signal cabins. A bath was even purchased for the stationmaster's house at Galashiels. There the 'Gentlemen's First Class Waiting Room', the booking office and hall saw 'improvements'. Alterations were also made to the station buildings at Hawick. Longer bogie carriages, first acquired by the NBR in 1885, resulted in extensions to platforms at Galashiels, Gorebridge and Hassendean. There were more sidings for Galashiels, Hardengreen and Fountainhall (the latter in connection with the new Lauder branch). Goods guards and shunters applied for macintosh overcoats, leggings and watches. They got the waterproofs but not the watches. There were innovations too – gas lighting, lavatories and steam heating in some carriages for First Class passengers. However, the NBR was severely criticised as 'an unpunctual railway', in fact the worst in Britain, hardly a recommendation for intending travellers.

In 1883 William, 10th Marquis of Tweeddale, became a director of the North British Railway. He was the owner of 40,000 acres of Border country and had served as a Liberal peer and politician. During his association with the NBR, the Light Railways Act of 1896 was passed. Prior to this, any new railway had to secure its own Act of Parliament for its construction – an expensive and lengthy exercise. The

The impressive lattice girder bridge at the north entrance to Bowshank tunnel, seen prior to its restoration, withstood the devastating flood of September 1891.

The inscribed stone at the north mouth of Bowshank tunnel recording the flood level that the Gala Water reached on 21 September 1891 – a flood of severity by which others are judged.

A former Drummond 4-4-0 tank engine, as LNER No.10425, waits at Fountainhall with a train of two former NBR six-wheelers as used on the Lauder branch in the 1920s.
(Glen Collection)

An advertisement in patriotic colours for the opening of the Lauder Light Railway on 2 July 1901.

(National Archives of Scotland)

revised legislation simplified the process of obtaining powers for a railway and thereby cut the cost of doing so.

A suggestion for a line to Lauder was first mentioned in 1847 and again in 1852. Ten years later came an offer to run a coach on behalf of the NBR between Lauder and Stow, and the railway company was prepared to pay a small subsidy of 11d (5p) a day. This gave a connection to the Waverley Route at Stow. But Lauder felt isolated although only 7 miles from Earlston (on the branch through Duns to Reston on the East Coast main line). There were only weekly carriers, one going north to Dalkeith and another south to Galashiels. Lauder was 26½ miles (42.6km) south of Edinburgh and a light railway would transform its accessibility.

An economic downturn in the early 1880s had adversely affected rural areas – light railways were seen as a solution to transport problems in districts of low population and little industry. A 'Light Railway Order' or 'LRO' permitted a small company to construct and operate a line. As the track was lightly laid, speeds and axle loads were limited. Level crossings had no gates but cattle grids were put in place, and there was little or no signalling as the principle was 'one engine in steam' only. Reductions in local rates were another inducement. However, the Act really came too late to be effective – the motorcar, bus and lorry would soon overtake the 'Light Railway' concept.

In 1883 when a railway was suggested between Lauder and Fountainhall, the NBR directors 'agreed to work the line

when constructed'. It was known to be an exposed route reaching over 944ft (287.7m), but the driver of the horse-drawn omnibus, trying to keep the road clear of snow, was refused extra payment by the NBR. So local agitation for a railway continued and that October a deputation 'waited on the Board' without success. The NBR directors soon had to reconsider their position as in 1887 the Marquis of Tweeddale became chairman, a position he held for several years. The Lauder Light Railway, 10½ miles (16.8km) long and climbing at 1 in 50 from Fountainhall, was on the agenda again. The circuitous line went over the hills flanking the Waverley Route on the east, and its 'LRO' was obtained on 30 June 1898.

The Marchioness of Tweeddale cut the first sod at Lauder on 3 June 1899. Being on the River Leader, this 'old but small Royal Burgh' was a popular venue with trout fishermen. When the branch opened on 2 July 1901, it had been constructed on a 'shoe string' for £38,911. There was only one intermediate station at Oxton. As there was no turntable at Lauder, engines had to run round their short trains and operate in reverse going back down to Fountainhall., a journey taking 47 minutes. The Lauder Light Railway maintained its independence as a company until 1923 when the LNER took over.

By no stretch of the imagination, were the Waverley Route or the Settle & Carlisle line suitable for non-stop running between London and Edinburgh. Nevertheless, in 1901, a 'show case' non-stop effort by the Midland and NBR companies took place. It aimed at press attention by offering a faster schedule than the *Flying Scotsman* service. The latter was then accelerated and the Midland-NBR train, even with the inducement of the latter's restaurant car, attracted few passengers, and soon ceased.

In 1902, with healthier finances, the NBR spent considerable sums on Hawick with a loading bank costing £1,889, and a coaling stage and sidings at £1,096. Galashiels saw investment of £3,918 in an engine shed and turntable east of the station. There were to be even more sidings at Falahill. Housing for the stationmaster at

The Lauder Light Railway made Fountainhall a junction, and here a former LMS Class 5, as BR No. 45368, heads a freight train on the Waverley Route where the Lauder branch veers right by the signal box. (J L Stevenson)

Fushiebridge and for surfacemen at Tynehead was to be provided, and the stationmaster's house at Eskbank 'improved'. St Boswells station would be rebuilt. Innovation was catching up with the NBR – signalling at Hawick would have electric track circuits while 'telephonic communication' would be available at Hardengreen. The latter had a significant role to play, regularly providing banking engines for the ascent of Borthwick Bank up to Falahill summit.

In July 1904, Borderers saw an exciting cavalcade on the railway – this was conveying Buffalo Bill's Wild West Show to many venues. Bill Cody was a colourful figure from the 'Old West' in the United States who became a famous showman. Three trains were specially chartered to take his Indians, cowboys and other performers to twenty-nine towns and cities across Scotland. The show, with its 200 horses and 22 buffalos in various re-enactments, was a huge attraction in Galashiels and Hawick. The NBR was responsible for its safe passage before it went onwards to Motherwell. Other 'cavalcades' were associated with the movement of circuses. The annual show for the Royal Highland & Agricultural Society also called for rail transport on a grand scale and Border towns were occasionally selected with Kelso, being a regular venue, and Hawick figuring once in 1914.

A public relations initiative, unusual for the NBR, had begun in 1892 whereby stationmasters were offered 'premiums' for best-kept stations. This involved station gardens, and by 1907, where the Borders Railway now runs, the competition was well established, Eskbank (Mr Bryce) and Stow (Mr Ward) both winning First Class prizes of £4. Smart stations typified the Waverley Route.

By the 1900s, new challenges were facing railway companies in Britain. Top of the list was the need for more powerful locomotives able to maintain faster schedules and to haul heavier trains. The Caledonian Railway was expecting 60mph running from its expresses between stations. Refinements in boiler performance, aimed at extracting as much energy as possible from the coal and water used, were leading to compounding and superheating technologies. Such developments could not be ignored by the directors of the North British Railway.

When the NBR was first constructed in the 1840s, John Miller had employed James Bell, a builder to trade, on the project. His work so impressed Miller that in time he became the company's resident engineer. His son joined the NBR as a youth, benefiting from the experience of family members who were managers and permanent way men. Bell succeeded his father as Engineer-in-Chief in 1897, at a time when that official had almost unlimited authority on a railway. Bell junior was no exception – he was

acknowledged as a specialist in permanent way and hailed as a devoted 'company servant'. He knew the NBR's network in detail – it had grown from 320 miles (515km) to roughly 1,380 miles (2,220km) during his service.

In 1905, Dr John Inglis joined the NBR board and he had a very different background. He was the son of the founder of the shipbuilding firm of A&J Inglis, established in 1862 at Pointhouse where the River Kelvin joins the Clyde. He became a noted engineer and shipbuilder, with an expertise in boilers for naval ships. Glasgow University conferred the honorary degree of Doctor of Laws for his contributions to engineering and to public life. He was also close to the NBR board, the Inglis yard having first built a vessel for the company in 1864; more recently several paddle steamers for its Clyde services had been completed – all of these carrying names from Sir Walter Scott's novels. (PS Waverley, now the world's last sea-going paddle steamer, was constructed by Inglis for the LNER in 1947).

Dr Inglis, being both observant and widely travelled, soon called for massive investment in new locomotives and carriages. Unlike the Caledonian and more progressive railway companies, the NBR did not renew one-thirtieth of its locomotive stock each year out of revenue. Consequently, it was simply being outclassed by its rivals. Even so, some directors were unconvinced, urging caution as in recent decades there had been substantial investment by the

With improving finances, the NBR invested in better facilities at Borders stations, and in 1902 Galashiels got a new engine shed and turntable east of its station.
(J L Stevenson Collection)

**Below left:** Banking engines from Hardengreen assisted heavy trains up Borthwick Bank to Falahill. Here a former NBR 0-6-0 gives such help in BR years.
(W S Sellar)

**Below:** A postcard from the late 1900s shows a NBR Atlantic No.879 *Abbotsford* approaching Carlisle on a train of 'Midland Scotch Joint Stock' bound for London St Pancras.
(Glen Collection)

An imposing and powerful engine, the former NBR Atlantic *Teribus*, as LNER No.9906, pauses at Eskbank in the 1920s. 'Teribus' is a name associated with Hawick, whose people are known as 'Teries'. (Glen Collection)

company – a third of the cost of the Forth Bridge, a new Tay Bridge, the line over Glenfarg, a revamped Waverley Station with its imposing hotel, the West Highland Railway and its extension, and Methil Docks for coal exports. All this was in addition to routine expenditure. Dr Inglis persisted and in November 1905 won agreement for the construction of Atlantic locomotives, 4-4-2s 'having four-coupled driving wheels with not more than 20 tons on each axle of the greatest power', to be ordered for passenger services. There would also be new 'block trains' or carriage sets, with dining cars and improved facilities for passengers. The new engines would have romanticised names taken from the places they would serve and the Borders were well represented – from '*Abbotsford*' and '*Borderer*' to '*Liddesdale*' and '*Teribus*'. This was an indication that they would work the Waverley Route with which they would become closely associated.

With drawings prepared by NBR staff, Dr Inglis invited tenders, and the North British Locomotive Company's offer of £4,525 per engine was accepted. There was then dissension – James Bell had apparently not been shown the design. It is said that he disliked the Atlantics on sight, found them 'top heavy' and worried about their effect on track. Hitherto, the biggest locomotives that the NBR had were 4-4-0s, considered best suited to its sinuous lines, especially through the Border country and through Fife. Yet Atlantic locomotives were well known on other companies' lines – the Great Northern Railway, an East Coast partner, having examples from 1898. The North Eastern had run its V class Atlantics on East Coast expresses into Edinburgh Waverley since 1903.

As many structures were now over fifty years old, Bell was concerned and wrote to the board. In response, he as 'Engineer-in-Chief' was instructed 'to carefully observe the state of the stone viaducts, adopt means to ensure safety and report from time to time to the Committee'. The NBR's new engines were delivered in the summer of 1906 and their introduction proved controversial, to say the least. There were no turntables big enough to accommodate them at Aberdeen, Carlisle or Dundee. Adverse reports soon came – first from the lightly constructed Arbroath-Montrose section. By December, it was the Waverley Route with 'alterations in the line and gauge of the railway between Hawick and Carlisle'. Broken rails (always reported to the directors) and track spread were attributed to the new Atlantics. Such outcomes convinced Bell that the locomotives were unsuitable for the route and he strongly recommended their withdrawal from it.

Many years before a decision was taken on Atlantic locomotives, there were concerns about coal extraction near the Waverley Route. In 1891 these had focussed on Dalhousie viaduct (now known as Lothianbridge) over the South Esk. Coal masters were no respecters of the railway and in 1878 the Gore Pit with a shaft 700ft deep had been sunk right beside the line at Gorebridge. Yet by 1900,

The extensive yards south of Newtongrange station served the Lady Victoria Colliery, seen on the right. A coal train is on the down line of the Waverley Route by the signal box in May 1970. (K M Falconer)

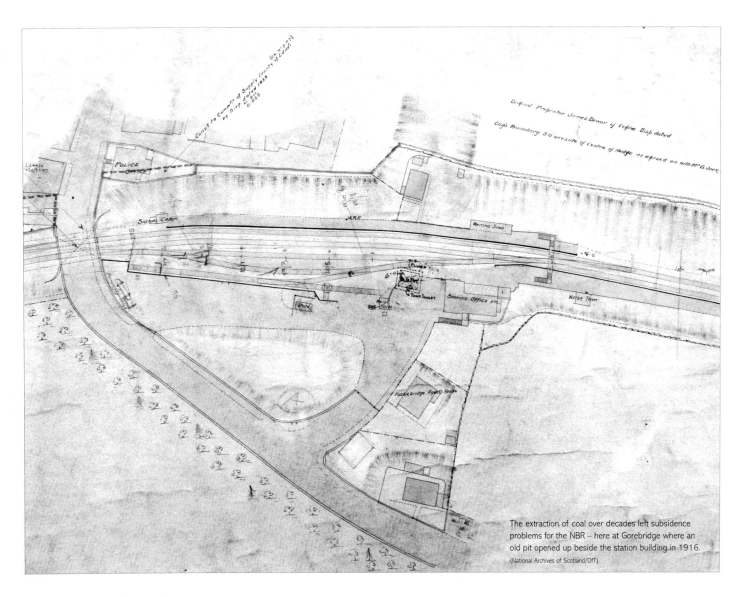

The extraction of coal over decades left subsidence problems for the NBR – here at Gorebridge where an old pit opened up beside the station building in 1916. (National Archives of Scotland/DfT)

despite the coal riches of the Lothians, over half the Scottish coal industry was located in Lanarkshire and only 5 per cent was in Mid- and East Lothian. The Esk basin, with numerous seams at depth and outcrops on its margins, soon became the target for much more investment in pits.

In 1890 when the Marquis of Lothian leased three pits to the Lothian Coal Company, a deep shaft going down to 1,624ft (495m) was sunk for an entirely new pit. This opened in 1895 and was named the Lady Victoria Colliery after his wife, but it was uncomfortably close to Dalhousie viaduct. However, there were severe problems with water in this pit – indeed, 5,000tons of water, equal to 2½ times the weight of coal raised per day – had to be pumped out, but this did not stop its expansion and early use of coal-cutting machinery. The workforce and their families were well housed in the 'model' settlement of nearby Newtongrange.

From 1905 Dalhousie viaduct appears regularly in NBR Minutes. It had been suspect from the start with a crack appearing on its tallest pier even before the Edinburgh & Hawick Railway had been completed. Now there were sufficient concerns for Bell's team responsible for 'New Works' to prepare plans for an entirely new structure. This modern viaduct would have had concrete piers (strengthened with old rail – a nod to NBR cost saving) faced with layers of 'best blue Staffordshire brick'. There

would be steel lattice girders on top to carry double tracks. The cost was put at £68,000. The reconstruction, 'in another position, in consequence of mineral workings there under', would mean 'a slight deviation in the line' to the west.

By March 1906, Bell was submitting letters about other viaducts. Dalhousie was not the only deficient structure on the system and soon attention was being given to Ratho

Newtongrange station, replacing Dalhousie, was opened in 1908 to serve the mining community there. (Glen Collection)

A section of the lattice girder design proposed for a replacement Lothianbridge (Dalhousie) viaduct by the NBR's Engineer-in-Chief in 1905. (National Archive of Scotland)

The low cost solution for Lothianbridge (Dalhousie) viaduct was to strengthen the arches and piers with bands of old bullhead rail as this early postcard shows. (Midlothian Archives and Local Studies)

Lothian Bridge, Newtongrange

(now Newbridge), Castlecary, Leaderfoot and South Esk – the latter on the Arbroath & Montrose Railway – in fact, any place that the Atlantics might run. With memories of the first Tay Bridge, NBR engineers had a horror of suspect structures that might collapse. In August 1907 agreement was reached between lawyers acting for the Marquis of Lothian and the NBR. In November the Lothian Coal Company stated its willingness to avoid extracting minerals that might 'endanger' Dalhousie viaduct during a lease extending to 1920. As compensation the railway had to pay the coal company £500 a year. A new structure was ruled out, and for Bell it was a case of 'make-do-and-mend' in NBR fashion with the old viaduct being strengthened at a cost of £12,000 – to be debited to revenue at £2,500 per half year.

So at Dalhousie, old bullhead rail was wrapped around the piers in bands and a 'cradle' of steel was inserted below track level. The 'intervals' in the piers that had contributed to the light appearance of the viaduct were infilled with

ashlar. Preliminary work saw the replacement of Dalhousie station southwards with 'Newtongrange', opened in August 1908, while two temporary signal boxes were installed – Dalhousie North and South. Sunday after Sunday there were engineering possessions, while on weekdays there was single line working and speed limits of 6mph in force.

Meantime, efforts were being made to improve the 'passenger experience' on the NBR. Steam heating was introduced and staff advised that 'Horse Boxes, Fish or Carriage Trucks, Yeast Vans and such like Vehicles' without steam pipes, must not be attached between the engine and carriages 'so as to sever the heating'. However, increased comfort on the NBR was tempered by economy in the use of gas, oil and other stores. In March 1907, a notice on the 'Discontinuance of Foot Warmers for the Season' appeared as usual. These were metal 'hot water bottles', filled with a sodium acetate solution that was heated in boilers at larger stations such as Hawick and placed in compartments. Regardless of the weather conditions, the foot warmers were 'forthwith withdrawn' and returned to St Margarets depot in Edinburgh. Consequently, travel rugs and heavy coats were advisable for journeys on the NBR.

For lighting, the company had progressed from oil lamps in 'pots' on carriage roofs to a gas system developed by Pintsch, a German chemist. This was piped into tanks beneath carriages at Edinburgh Waverley but was highly flammable. By the 1900s, trains could be lit by electric light supplied from batteries below the carriages – but this was only to be switched on when 'absolutely necessary' and although 'full light in tunnels' was permitted, this must be immediately turned off on leaving.

The introduction of the Atlantics probably hastened further bridge renewals – two under bridges were replaced between Galashiels and Melrose in November 1907, while Torwoodlee bridge was also partially renewed. In 1908, repairs to the bridge at the north end of Bowshank tunnel and work on structures between Bowland and Stow were reported. Leaderfoot viaduct on the Kelso branch was also strengthened and Whitrope tunnel given attention. The Engineer-in-Chief and his team were certainly kept busy.

Of the big increase in output from the Lothian collieries in the 1900s over 70 per cent was exported from South Leith, mainly to Scandinavia and the Baltic. In return, imports of agricultural products and timber flowed into Central Scotland. Capacity on both railway and harbour was inadequate, with the line from Portobello to the quaysides a bottleneck. Lothian coal owners were angered by the frequent delays, the lame excuses and the excessive charges that the NBR made for its poor service.

Matters came to a head in 1912 when the coal owners took action. They determined to break the NBR's monopoly and develop a faster route to the Forth. A Bill was framed seeking parliamentary approval for their Lothian Railway, a system that would be completely independent. The line, linking various feeder collieries in Midlothian, would run for over 12 miles on Edinburgh's southeast flank to the Forth. There a long causeway would stretch into the firth towards Seafield. The railway would operate on a similar basis to the canals of old – the coal owners providing their own engines and wagons and paying for the use of the rail system.

The NBR directors were incensed by this scheme and opposed it. The Bill failed but only after the company promised to improve its existing routes to make them capable of handling the volume of coal traffic. The NBR therefore had to promote its own Lothian lines, with a

In the 1900s when the NBR set about improving the 'passenger experience', this 12-wheel dining carriage proved a profitable venture. (North British Railway Study Group)

smaller mileage, authorised in August 1913. This was mostly single track, but the civil engineering was heavy and expensive with testing curves and gradients. Both the East Coast main line and the Waverley route had to be crossed. At the same time, dock access was upgraded, and as branches proliferated, the entire Lothian coalfield benefited from a complex of lines. The First World War spurred the project on and by September 1915, coal trains were rumbling over the tracks by day and night.

Between 1898 and 1902, the South African War had been fought, a conflict in which the King's Own Scottish Borderers, a local regiment, had taken part. When the Stobs estate south of Hawick came up for sale in 1902, it was bought by the War Office to provide training facilities for the Army. There was already a station at Stobs itself, but when camp construction began in 1903, a railway siding off the Waverley Route was formed at Acreknowe farm. A narrow gauge line was laid into the camp. Some buildings were set up, including an Officers' Mess and an Institute for the YMCA, but the intention was that Stobs would be used primarily as a summer training ground for volunteer territorial units, the men being provided only with tents. The Camp Commander and his staff meanwhile would be accommodated in Stobs Castle. When the volunteer units were transformed into the Territorial Force in 1908, Stobs Camp became a well known destination for men from all over Scotland, with an annual camp being held for a fortnight each summer to improve training.

Tensions between Britain and the German Empire had been increasing in the 1900s, with bitter rivalries on the high seas and in Africa as the nations vied for imperial power. The British Empire was now represented on every inhabited continent and the Royal Navy protected its interests worldwide. The British government's intention was to maintain a 'two power' fleet – a navy at least twice as big and powerful as that of any other two nations together. A programme for building warships, known as 'Dreadnoughts', was begun in 1906 and generated a vast demand for boilerplate from Northern England. This involved 'out of gauge' loads, conveyed by the NBR on Sundays over the Waverley Route. No trains were allowed to pass and any 'tight fit' locations, such as tunnels, had to be taken slowly. The heavy trains made their way to Clyde shipyards via Edinburgh's South Suburban line and Bathgate.

In 1912, with the international situation worsening, the British government formed a Railway Executive Committee from the general managers of the main railway companies. This was with a view to co-ordinating services in the event of war when the government would then take control of the railways using the existing managements to carry out its policies.

The outbreak of the First World War on 4 August 1914 signalled the end of an era.

The conflict would bring weighty responsibilities to the NBR as 'Secretary Company' in Scotland, involving liaison with other Scottish railway companies, with the military authorities and with Scottish Command. On the instruction 'all other traffic must stand aside', many expresses and other passenger services were immediately withdrawn and excursion trains ceased. Those for the government now had priority as the nation went to war. The NBR forthwith intensified its traffic operations for the movement of troop trains and freight for military purposes. It also fitted up an ambulance train for the reception of casualties. Government traffic had to be carried without charge or the submission of accounts – post-war, compensation would be paid to the railway companies, plus interest at 4 per cent on new capital expended on any essential projects since January 1913.

**Below:** An advertisement for the Lothian Coal Company at Galashiels whose wagon loads supplied the mills in the town with fuel for raising steam. (A A Boyd)

**Bottom:** A typical Lothians coal train hauled by a former NBR 0-6-0 locomotive, as LNER No.9627. with the name 'Pétain' commemorating its service in France in the First World War. (W S Sellar)

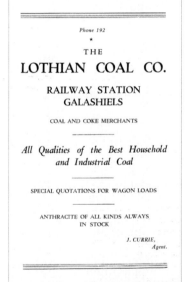

A postcard sent in 1904 shows the pipe band of a Highland territorial battalion beside North British carriages on a siding at Stobs Camp, near Hawick.
(Derek Robertson Collection)

In every town in the Borders, territorial forces were mobilised. The King's Own Scottish Borderers had wide support and soon troops were being mustered at drill halls and railway stations, hundreds were in transit on trains, and the NBR was at full stretch. Hawick was said to have 5,000 men looking for billets and an influx of Belgian refugees had also to be found shelter. At Galashiels, over 1,000 men were seeking lodgings. Large buildings, from church halls to mill warehouses, were requisitioned as temporary accommodation. Men from squadrons of the Lothians and Border Horse Yeomanry also gathered at local stations and many horses were commandeered from farms, hunts and local businesses. Throughout 1915, Stobs Camp became a centre for mobilisation and training for many Scottish regiments and for volunteers from Newfoundland. The NBR had to run numerous trains to and from Stobs, which later was used for prisoners of war.

Railway employees were enlisting in such numbers that restraint had to be placed on them doing so – otherwise the network simply could not have been run. Consequently, railwaymen became exempt from conscription. The conflict was not over by Christmas 1914, and it would put the railway under immense strain for five years. The Borders and Lothians buzzed with rumours about spies. Due to the threat of invasion, railwaymen were warned that all means of transport were to be removed or destroyed if instructions should be issued to that effect. Every employee might have to be a saboteur whether in a depot or out on the line. This was a dreadful thought as many enginemen doted on their locomotives, and stationmasters on their stations. The

Border mills were working flat out weaving khaki cloth and tartan for uniforms, canvas for tents, making blankets, and tons of knitted goods from balaclavas to stockings. Much production was sent out over the Waverley Route in NBR goods vans.

The return of disabled soldiers made the horrors of war only too plain. The Gallipoli campaign – a second 'Flodden' – and the battles of the Somme in 1915 took a terrible toll on Border families. Efforts were redoubled in communities to raise money for the Red Cross, for war hospitals and for parcels of 'comforts' to send to the troops. The NBR played its part in carrying such packages and 'flag days' were held at its stations. It sent 25 of its Class C goods locomotives to France for 'ROD' service – to assist the Railway Operating Division in hauling supplies to the front line. On their return, the engines were given names linked to the war – 'Maude' (named after a general) is now preserved in the Scottish Railway Museum at Bo'ness.

In response to the shortage of shells in 1915, a government factory for the manufacture of the explosive 'Cordite' was constructed at Gretna. This covered hundreds of acres and its narrow gauge railway was 125 miles long. Production began in April 1916 and soon 11,000 women were employed – twice as many as men.

A branch off the Waverley Route at Longtown served the facility, and for two years, the NBR transported over 70,000 tons of munitions from its sidings. It was dangerous work with high earnings. Wages rose generally, with war bonuses being paid to railway and other workers but so did the cost of living. Rail fares went up by 50 per cent, except for those engaged in the war effort.

'Daylight Saving Time', introduced in 1916, was explained as helpful to farmers who were being asked to produce as much food as possible. The NBR urged employees to use land around stations and signal boxes for growing crops – even slopes of embankments and cuttings were considered suitable. Some foods became scarce, and early in 1918, rationing for sugar, then for butter and meat, became compulsory.

With the intense wartime pressures, the NBR must have hoped for no interruptions to its network. However, the approach to Galashiels station from the west was below a steep bank where the rock was weak. First came the short Ladhope tunnel, followed by a tall brick retaining wall to support the slope. This had been reinforced on several occasions with buttresses and steel rail. On 14 December 1916, cracks were observed in the wall and it was seen to move. Workmen were on site attempting to make emergency repairs when there was a massive landslip and 70yds (63m) collapsed. This buried the double track in hundreds of tons of rock. Thankfully, the workmen escaped injury and a train just arrived from Peebles was unscathed. The line was blocked for several days, but the NBR provided a motorcar service between Bowland and Galashiels on the Waverley Route, and between Clovenfords and Galashiels on the Peebles branch. The wall, which still stands, had to be completely rebuilt.

As the war intensified, as many as 90 per cent of the active men in the Borders had either enlisted or were on reserve lists and women took on new roles in agriculture and industry. A social revolution was in progress. Early in 1917 the Scottish Women's Land Army was formed. German prisoners-of-war, housed at Stobs Camp, supplemented labour on farms and were paid 4 shillings (20p) a week. On the railway, with the shortage of men,

A view of Stobs Camp with volunteers accommodated 'under canvas' during summer training prior to huts being erected in the First World War.
(J L Stevenson Collection)

**Above:** Longtown, a wayside station on the Waverley Route, was near the junction for Gretna giving access to the immense munitions factory that was constructed there in the First World War. (J L Stevenson Collection)

**Above right:** The North British Railway was the key liaison for the Scottish railway companies with the military in the First World War. Its coat of arms showed the crests of Edinburgh and Glasgow. (Wikipedia)

**Right:** A collpase of the Ladhope Wall close to Galashiels station in December 1916 called for round-the-clock efforts to clear the tracks and get trains running again. The wall was then rebuilt. (Glen Collection)

**Below:** Comrades in arms – were these men NBR employees who joined up in the First World War? They were photographed at Galashiels station with other members of staff beside a Scott class 4-4-0 No.897 *Redgauntlet*. (National Archives of Scotland/DfT)

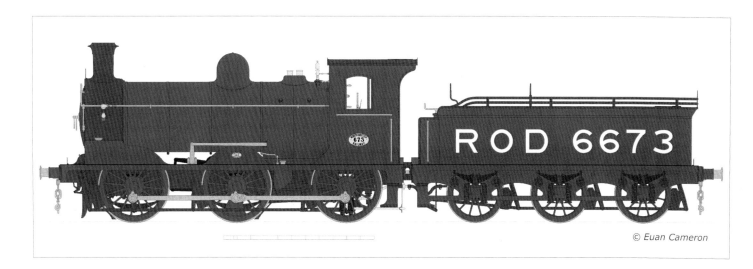

© Euan Cameron

The North British Railway gave 25 locomotives of its Class C 0-6-0s to the Railway Operating Division for service in France. This artist's impression shows ROD No.6673 that was named *Maude* after a general on its return. This engine has been preserved. (Euan Cameron)

The Waverley Route was under severe pressure in wartime with troop and other military specials, but after 1918 the 'Midland Scotch Joint Stock' could run again on expresses, here hauled by a NBR Scott class No.400 *The Dougal Cratur*. (R W Lynn)

women were employed in both clerical and manual work, such as cleaning locomotives at engine sheds. In 1914 there had been fewer than 120 women in NBR employment, mostly as clerks or cleaners, but by 1918 the number had risen more than tenfold.

From May 1917, a naval special was run every day from London conveying personnel to Rosyth, Invergordon, and Thurso for transit from there to Scapa Flow, the main base for the Grand Fleet. Out and back from Carlisle, this long train of 14 vehicles travelled over the Waverley Route, taking 21½ hours for the complete journey to and from London. Only officers had sleeping accommodation, hence this train earned the name 'The Misery' from other ranks. By that year, the NBR was coping with prodigious quantities of mail, coal, minerals and supplies for military and civilian use. Even although its peacetime passenger services had been almost halved, the company had been forced to construct extra locomotives and rolling stock.

With the conflict continuing, the losses were devastating. In 1914, at the outbreak of the war, the NBR's employees numbered 24, 625 but one out of every five enlisted. When peace came in November 1918, one in every sixteen of these had been lost. The effect on the railway and on the communities it served would be profound and long lasting. In the Borders, the sacrifice of active men, in the cause of a nation's freedom, would weigh heavily on its families, with successions in businesses, on farms and estates broken.

There would be no 'going back to normal' for the NBR or the Waverley Route in the post-war years. Uncertain times had begun. Would that company, always sparing with its money and now looking for compensation, be able to continue?

# Through Troubled Times

Throughout the First World War, the railway companies were under government direction and run as one entity during the national emergency. There were arguments in favour of maintaining state control in the post-war years and trade union opinion had long supported 'nationalisation'. Was this the time to buy out the private companies? For most managements and shareholders, this was a step too far.

By the time the Armistice came in November 1918, the railways were much depleted as both maintenance and replacements had been deferred. Apart from war priorities, to serve dock yards and munitions factories, investment had dried up. Consequently, the government proposed a scheme of amalgamation for the private railway companies, the intention being to 'secure economy of operation and increase efficiency of administration'. The board of the North British Railway considered this proposal unconstitutional – stating that it was 'impossible to suggest a greater violation of the rights of British subjects'. It was argued that the five Scottish networks should form one system but the Railway Companies' Association, charged with resolving the matter of compensation for each company, was unable to reach an agreement. The NBR held out for what its chairman William Whitelaw believed was a just settlement for its financial shortfalls. With a wealthy Glasgow background and well educated (Harrow and Cambridge), he was an MP as a young man, then served on railway company boards from 1898. By 1912 he was leading the NBR.

Hopes of pre-war 'normality' were an illusion as strikes and unrest were signs of painful readjustments. On 1 February 1919 the Railway Executive imposed a 48 hour week with an 8 hour day, and though such measures were long desired they did not quell distrust – there was a strike that September. Yet by 1920 the railway in the Borders was reporting its best year ever, with Galashiels and Hawick topping the list. Transporting livestock was a crucial element of NBR business, with St Boswells recording over 275,000 head and Hawick over 268,000 that year. Sadly, such positive returns would not last.

| NBR 1920 | Passenger tickets | Passenger revenue | Goods revenue | Total revenue |
|---|---|---|---|---|
| Galashiels | 274,442 | £41,781 | £42,376 | £84,157 |
| Hawick | 127,845 | £46,286 | £44,230 | £90,516 |
| Jedburgh Branch | | | | £21,126 |
| Selkirk Branch | | | | £34,914 |

– John Thomas, Vol.6 Scotland, The Lowlands and the Borders (1984)

A Railways Act of 1921, to take effect from 1 January 1923, forced 'a systematic, compulsory amalgamation scheme', devised by the government, on thirty-seven private railway companies in Britain. The grouping into the 'Big Four' – the Great Western, London & North Eastern (LNER), the London, Midland & Scottish (LMSR) and the Southern – took place, but not without protest. There would be no 'Scottish Railways'. The dominance of the East and West Coast main lines in the British transport system was considered of such significance that, as far as Scotland was concerned, two companies took control – the LNER with an East Coast focus, combined the North British and the Great North of Scotland Railways, while the LMSR on the West Coast absorbed the Caledonian, the Glasgow & South Western and the Highland Railway companies. Viewed from an international perspective, this was unusual – the companies remained privately owned and were not dependent on public subsidy, unlike the state systems in many other countries.

William Whitelaw, the chairman of the North British Railway, who became the chairman of the LNER on the amalgamtions of the private companies in 1923. (Church of Scotland)

The Waverley Route was now under the LNER and was soon seen as a 'secondary main line'. The NBR's 'partner company', the Midland Railway, owner of the Settle & Carlisle line, became part of the LMSR. However, this arrangement left the passenger timetable of day and overnight trains between Edinburgh Waverley and London St Pancras via the pre-Grouping routes largely unchanged. There were two daytime trains and an overnight sleeper, services that Border businessmen found convenient. By contrast, in England, the former Midland line had principally played an 'inter city' role serving Leeds, Sheffield, Derby, Nottingham and other centres. The effect of the company groupings on goods traffic was complex as such movements involved wagon loads, with Carlisle being a key centre for exchanging these. Consignments of woollens or cloth from Galashiels or Hawick bound for southern markets were usually sent out in vans as 'sundries' or as parcels.

The transition to what was seen as 'London control' was far from welcome among Scottish railwaymen. For many, the old North British – in spite of its deficiencies – was more than a job, it was a way of life. It was not unusual for fifty years' service to be devoted to a railway company and loyalties could be intense. Instructions now came, not only from Edinburgh, but also from south of the border – Darlington, Doncaster and York figuring on official letters.

The modern logo that became a design icon for the LNER. (Glen Collection)

An old map showing the extensive system that the LNER took over from the North British, Great North of Scotland and North Eastern Railway Companies.

(Glen Collection)

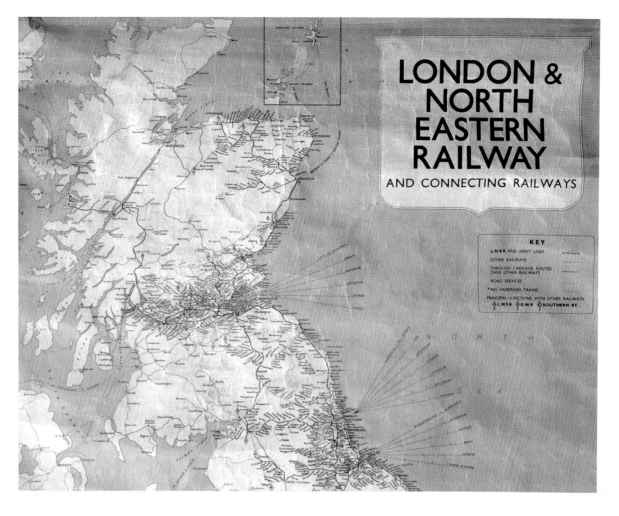

There were new policies, new methods of working and new uniforms. The 'bronze green' for passenger engines and the claret carriages of the NBR were 'out'. In addition to renumbering, locomotives and new rolling stock had new liveries – apple green for passenger engines, black for the rest, while coaching stock was varnished teak.

There was some satisfaction when William Whitelaw, the North British chairman, was given the same position in the LNER, an appointment which he held until 1938. Described as 'astute, enterprising and tactful', his claim was indisputable as he had wide experience of both the political and railway scene. The LNER had a decentralised approach to governance that gave Scotland a general manager and a local board of directors.

Although covering a large area, and having the second largest route mileage in Britain, the LNER was economically weak. In 1923, it was the leading coal railway hauling over 100 million tons, but such tonnages were soon in sharp decline and this would hit its revenue hard. In the 1920s and 30s, its industrial heartland in England's North East, dependent on coal mining, iron, steel and heavy industry, became a seriously depressed region with high unemployment.

Given financial uncertainties, rural branch lines were a headache for railway managements and steam railcars were an attempt to introduce an economical method of working them. A company, with the brand name 'Sentinel' and Glasgow origins, was set up in Shrewsbury in 1906, and became well known for steam road wagons. At the British Empire Exhibition of 1924, Nigel Gresley, Chief Mechanical Engineer of the LNER, saw a Sentinel railcar on display. It seemed commodious and cheaper to run than a locomotive-hauled train. A railcar was tested by the LNER, pronounced a success, and 80 Sentinel steam railcars, were purchased between 1925 and 1932. In the Borders, these 'steam coaches' in cream and green livery, soon appeared on the Langholm and Selkirk branches. A driver-stoker, plus a guard-conductor, were needed, but many crews found them temperamental – there was either plenty of steam, or there was none. Boys liked to travel on them:

'Like a bus, the aisle was lined with leather straps for

The Sentinel railcar *Pearl* at Carlisle station in 1929 when operating on branch line services to Langholm and to Silloth. (R W Lynn)

Galashiels station in the 1920s when motor vehicles were appearing in growing numbers. The station had many enamel signs displayed on its walls.
(R W Lynn)

standing passengers, but it was much more fun to copy Tarzan and swing the length of the coach strap by strap…'
    – James Turnbull in 'Southern Annual', 164.

The cost of frequent repairs, together with the Second World War, led to their withdrawal by 1945.

In 1926 came the General Strike when the whole country was brought almost to a standstill. Some railwaymen and staff, with the assistance of volunteers, tried to keep a limited train service running. After only nine days most strikers returned to work, but the miners stayed 'out' for months and coal became scarce. The episode left a residue of resentment in union circles, and railwaymen, who often had strong loyalties to one another, had to face tensions at work. In the aftermath, the LNER reduced staff numbers, and those employees retained had to accept cuts of 2½ per cent in salaries and wages, with no increase for two years.

As the railway companies were dominated by directors and managements for whom out-competing rival companies had been a basic philosophy, such attitudes initially underpinned the provision of both passenger and freight services. However, the railways would be severely challenged by new transport modes – the motorcar, bus and lorry. (The NBR had motorcar services before the First World War, and it also bought war surplus lorries). During the conflict, there were technological advances in motor vehicles with servicemen becoming familiar with their operation and maintenance. Post war, surplus lorries enabled veterans to set up haulage businesses and, being exempt from rail freight pricing – where rates were published – their lower charges took goods away from the railways.

Soon bus services offering cheaper fares, better frequencies and more flexible routes, were competing with rural branch lines. In 1921 the first bus service from Galashiels to Selkirk was introduced by Brook & Amos. In the hinterlands of rural stations, villages were targeted by such operators; a bus service between Selkirk and Hawick, taking 30 minutes instead of an hour by rail, really hurt passenger traffic. Almost in step with these developments, the streets in Galashiels were being surfaced with tar macadam and the 'horse drinking fountain' in Market Street

removed. Garages, for car sales and servicing, plus petrol pumps, soon appeared. There was a similar pattern in other Border towns.

From the early 1920s, closures of stations and cessations of passenger services were under discussion by the LNER. This was potentially cost saving, reducing the wages bill, as passenger stations required three staff – stationmaster, booking clerk and porter. Nevertheless, Whitelaw and the LNER board were at pains to keep lines open for freight in the hope of an upturn in trade. Stations and structures became shabby as even basic maintenance and re-painting had cost implications.

Although the LNER was struggling to pay dividends, the board had aspirations – speed and comfort. Nigel Gresley and his teams produced new designs for locomotives, and in 1924 'Flying Scotsman' was displayed at the British Empire Exhibition at Wembley. This was the first of the LNER Pacifics that broke records and caught the public eye. However, no engines would be designed specifically for the difficult Waverley Route with its curves and hills. Its services were hauled by former NBR 4-4-0s, the 'Scotts', 'Intermediates' and 'Glens', plus the redoubtable 'Atlantics'. To the LNER, the latter class was 'non-standard', had seen hard usage and in 1933 the first withdrawals took place. The J36 and J37 classes of 0-6-0s, the 'maids of all work'

Glenesk Junction was where the Dalkeith line took off from the Waverley Route; it closed to passengers in 1942 and to goods in 1964. (W S Sellar)

In 1924 a class of 4-4-0 locomotives were assigned to Scotland and took names from the writings of Sir Walter Scott. Here LNER No.6398 *The Laird of Balmawhipple* is seen at Eastfield. (Glen Collection)

for freight duties and banking, plus various tank engines for local and yard workings, continued in service.

Only in1927 were A3 Pacifics, named after racehorse winners, allocated to Edinburgh's St Margarets and to Carlisle Canal depots. Such locomotives, with big driving wheels, were designed for fast running on straight, near level lines – not for tortuous tracks with steep gradients such as the Waverley Route. With an eye on publicity, the name 'The Thames-Forth Express' was conferred on a daily train with a 'Pullman Restaurant' each way, bringing a dash of glamour to the route.

That year, O S Nock, the distinguished railway author, first sampled the Waverley Route northbound while travelling on the footplate of the Atlantic No.9873 *St Mungo*. He knew Britain's main lines well and wrote:

*'In no possible stretch of the imagination could one consider this wild, fascinating, heavily graded railway as a fast express route ...'* – Main Lines across the Border

A call at Steele Road on the Waverley Route in 1961 for BR No.60043 *Brown Jack*, three of whose sister engines had been allocated to Carlisle Canal in 1927. (Stuart Sanders)

(1960)

He advised any doubters to look at the gradient profile to appreciate the problems – a climb of 1 in 75 for 8 miles from Newcastleton up to Whitrope Summit that he judged worse than Beattock. Going south, from the platform end at Hawick, the start was at 1 in 75, with much climbing at or close to that grade up to Whitrope. Southbound from Edinburgh, there was the gruelling ascent 8 miles long at 1 in 70 from Hardengreen up to Falahill. Even with powerful engines in good shape, it was a slog often at less than 30 mph up the hills on heavy trains. It was a punishing assignment for the A3s.

Furthermore, the Waverley Route had the most continuous curvature of any main line anywhere in the country. Going downhill, drivers had to do the best they could, being mindful of the curves and speed restrictions, and there were few straights to ease the strain. On the footplate, the big engines swayed first right, then left, then right again, as reverse curves followed one another – some with checkrail, all having to be taken cautiously. Yet the Atlantics were capable of logging just under two hours for the hard 98 miles 15 chains(158km) between Edinburgh and Carlisle.

Road competition became increasingly intense. In the Borders and Lothians, buses were being operated by the SMT – the Scottish Motor Traction Company Ltd, established in Edinburgh in 1905. The LNER tried to win back custom in 1927 by promoting 'Cheap Return Fares' on Edinburgh and Galashiels trains – with no luggage allowed, but offering 'Speed & Comfort by Rail'. In 1929 after legislation permitted railway companies to run buses, the LNER and the LMSR both acquired a stake in SMT. A year later, SMT began an Edinburgh-London coach service that took two days but was cheaper than going by rail.

Compared with bus operators and road hauliers, regulatory systems weighed heavily on railway companies. A severe handicap was the obligation to be a 'Common Carrier' as laid down by Parliament, to publish rates and avoid selective discounts. Railways charged on the basis of a commodity's value rather than on the cost of handling the

On an excursion train in April 1965, A4 BR No.60031 *Golden Plover* negotiates the notorious curves of the Waverley Route near Riccarton Junction, seen far left. (ColourRail)

item, and it was feared by railway companies that raising freight prices would lead to further losses of traffic. Meanwhile, road hauliers were taking higher value goods and leaving the 'low margin' bulk to the railways. It seemed manifestly unfair – road transport did not have to finance its infrastructure, had no commitments to trade unions, and was free from regulation. Only in 1930 was a licensing system for buses set up, with one for freight following in 1933 – but no restrictions were placed on traders' own vehicles and these posed the biggest threat to the railways.

In addition to the many branch lines in the Borders, the LNER was saddled with a secondary main line no longer perceived as 'picturesque' or 'romantic'. By the mid-1920s, modern authors were in vogue and the writings of Sir Walter Scott were out of fashion. In a holiday context, the region now had limited promotional possibilities. Although there were stretches of high moorland and pastoral landscapes with woodlands, there was no Ben Nevis, Monessie Gorge

or lochs, beside the line, and the terrain was certainly not 'Royal Deeside' or 'The Trossachs'. In addition, the route went through drab and often smoky mill towns, altogether too industrial to promote as holiday venues. It had no seaside resort as a focus for holidaymakers. Moreover, it was as ever a slow route at a time when the LNER was concentrating its efforts on trains that were exceptionally fast and well appointed. Although Abbotsford appeared on a poster, what was also chosen for the Waverley Route by the LNER's talented advertising department were the Border abbeys of both Dryburgh and Melrose. Jointly with the LMS, Carlisle, an unlikely choice, became 'The Holiday Centre for Romantic Borderland and Lakelands'.

The inter-war peak for railways in Britain was in 1929 when there were 642,000 employees, 1,237 million passengers were carried and 300 million tons of goods were transported, but this was only strength on paper. Profitability was weak and the companies' capital structure adversely affected performance. As much as 75 per cent of their capital was 'fixed interest', consisting of debentures and preference stock that had first call for interest payments. In some instances in the bad times, such dividends were paid out of reserves while ordinary shareholders got nothing. Meanwhile, rail unions complained of pay cuts and deteriorating working conditions for their members.

**Below left:** The Scott Country and Abbotsford were not forgotten by the LNER as this 1930 poster of the Borders landscape shows. (Science & Society Picture Library)

**Below:** A tempting offer from the LNER? Cheap return fares between Galashiels and Edinburgh 'off peak' via Peebles in 1927. (Glen Collection)

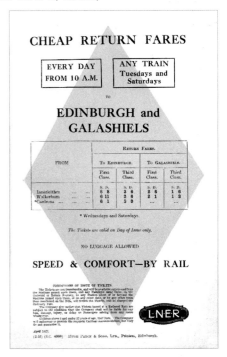

With the Wall Street crash of 1929 the hopes of better economic circumstances were dashed. Britain was plunged into financial chaos, causing industrial shut downs and prolonged unemployment in Scotland and the North of England. The Borders were badly affected. By 1933, the worldwide depression was taking its grip and three Gala mills – Botany, Netherdale and Tweed – closed that year; Abbots Mill and Midmill followed in 1935. This had a knock-on effect on related activities, including the railway and despite the licensing restrictions placed on road haulage in 1933, volumes of rail freight continued to shrink.

With so much industry at a standstill, the private railway companies were in a precarious financial position, and the LNER was brought 'perilously close to bankruptcy'. Some contraction was inevitable. The Lauder branch closed to passengers on 12 September 1932 (and to freight on 1 October 1958) and the line from Kelso Junction east to Roxburgh was singled in 1933. Attempts were made to sustain passenger interest with special excursions; the LNER appealed to mill workers by offering trips to Whitley Bay and Newcastle, while tours to the Borders visited Galashiels, Melrose, St Boswells, Hawick, or Selkirk – such trains having the attraction of a restaurant car. In 1933 the LNER organised 'The Northern Belle', a luxury tour of its Scottish lines, including the Waverley Route. This took passengers from London to 'See the Beauties of Scotland in Comfort' for a week. With first class rail travel, accommodation and meals, it cost £20.

Owning a motorcar was a widely held ambition. Cars – once custom built and very expensive – became 'affordable' for professionals, managers, and well-to-do farmers. Such makes as Austin and Morris rolled off southern production lines by the thousand. In Border towns where horses and carts had once stood, lorries and vans were now parked and there were more showrooms selling cars, and garages

servicing them, than ever. The LNER even advertised its willingness to take cars by rail at 3d a mile, thereby saving motorists 'road fatigue'.

By 1937, being well aware of the fundamental problems facing Britain's railways, William Whitelaw advocated state ownership for them. This would have combined fourteen groups and have included road transport. With the private shareholders bought out, the government would then set up a controlling body of experts in rail and road transport, similar to that of the London Transport Board.

As the LNER had only limited means, it invested in modest schemes that were aimed at cost saving. For example, in Galashiels in 1937 a modern colour light signalling system, controlled from a single signal box, replaced five old boxes. The new system covered an area from Kilnknowe Junction to Selkirk Junction with 'searchlight' signals electrically operated. The lines were track circuited with the position of trains being shown on an illuminated diagram. Siemens was responsible for this installation that modernised operations and improved safety, but staff numbers were reduced.

Although the doors of signal boxes carried the notice 'Strictly No Admittance', many of these were where men and boys went for haircuts. Signalmen were not only adept at 'short back and sides', they were often 'first with the news'. The boxes had wide views over their surroundings and good communications when few people had access to a telephone, and the signal boxes and their staffs were much missed.

At Galashiels, the old station bridge with its 25ft carriageway was inadequate for motor traffic and it was replaced with a new bridge opened in June 1938. As the Town Council also protested about the neglected state of the station, its entrance, roof and platforms were refurbished, the purpose being to update the buildings,

The Lauder branch closed to passengers in 1932, but freight continued with this former GER engine running with a tender to convey water, and empty side tanks to reduce the axle weight on the light railway. (E M Morten)

refresh their appearance and reduce maintenance.

Some recovery in the performance of the railways was beginning to show by 1937 although investment in railway stock was only half as profitable as returns on hotel investments. In 1932 the SMT group had bought the Dryburgh Arms Hotel near St Boswells, and whereas, excursionists had formerly looked to the railway for tours, many now turned to bus companies for itineraries 'off the beaten track' – and at less expense.

The railway tried to retain its goods and parcels traffic and there were some innovations. Advertisements now read, 'Send your goods by road rail container', a new demountable system, with similar facilities available for household removals. Borders stations continued to handle Royal Mail, newspapers and parcels, while goods yards took care of coal, now joined by petroleum as a fuel, bales of wool, general merchandise, and fruit. Livestock was transported from the fortnightly markets at Hawick and St Boswells, but motor lorries were already appearing in that trade. Faced with continuing tough competition for freight, the railway companies again argued for 'a level playing field' and in 1938 launched their campaign for 'A Square Deal'. This asked that railways be freed from regulated charges, permitting them to set their own rates. Though accepted by the government of the day, the tense international situation caused a deferral.

When the Second World War began on 3 September 1939, the railways again came under immediate government control. A new Executive Committee was established to operate the companies as one unit. As before, troop trains and military supplies were given priority. In the early months of 1939, the Department of Health in Scotland had prepared a plan for the evacuation of mothers with children, invalids and the blind, from areas likely to be vulnerable to aerial attack. The cities of Edinburgh, Glasgow and Dundee, plus strategic locations such as Rosyth, Inverkeithing and Clydebank, were priorities for this great dispersal of population. Evacuation was voluntary and some families made their own arrangements. For others, accommodation was requested and local reception committees formed.

When the order came on 31 August 1939 to 'Evacuate Forthwith', over 175,000 British children left home over three days in the 3,000 special trains that were scheduled to take them to the sanctuary of the countryside. Some saw the event as a great adventure, but for others it was profoundly upsetting. Many Edinburgh children went to the Borders, and LNER staff had to tackle the 'logistical nightmare' of transporting them there to the homes of local families. By Christmas 1939, with the threat of 'blitzkrieg' diminished, three-quarters of the evacuees had gone home. For the others, they had to adapt to Borders schools and rural routines.

Meanwhile, the Railway Executive had taken control of all aspects of operations. All signage that might assist an invader was removed. Station advertising 'in the national interest' used information boards for essential messages – about air raid protection or service provision. Timetables were radically revised, and although trains were lengthened, they became very congested. Stations were subject to 'black out', with no lights after dark. On locomotives, a heavy sheet was used to cover the footplate, preventing glare from the fire revealing the position of a depot or a train, but making conditions torrid for the crews. At stations, no matter how small or remote, strips of gummed paper were pasted on

**Top:** Some limited improvements by the LNER resulted in colour light signalling and a new signal box being installed at Galashiels in 1938 when the station was also refurbished. (Glen Collection)

**Above:** The Galashiels signal box was spotless, a railway tradition of pride in the job, and here signalman Adam Paton is in charge in 1968. (G Kinghorn)

This aerial view of Galashiels on the eve of the Second World War in 1939 shows a profusion of mills in the town and part of the large railway yards (lower right). (RCAHMS)

Postwar, a former LNER V2 with a freight train approaches Kilnknowe Junction, with the once busy Peebles branch on the left. (G Kinghorn)

windows to prevent damage from splintered glass, and sandbags were laid around doors to counter bomb blast. With manpower becoming scarce, women worked at engine sheds and station yards – at Riccarton Junction, they were soon cleaning out smoke boxes, a filthy job.

Air Raid Protection or 'ARP' wardens patrolled the towns and also checked on country locations to ensure that no lights showed after sun down. Fireguard duties were practised, as were ambulance routines in which railway staff took part. Everyone carried a gas mask. Stations such as Hawick, or junctions such as Galashiels or St Boswells, were considered vulnerable to aerial attack and were within range of hostile aircraft. Galashiels residents heard the flight overhead of enemy aircraft when Clydeside was blitzed in March 1941.

Once more, the factories and mills of the Border towns were in full production making textiles and woollens to clothe the forces. The railway was the artery that carried coal to keep steam power operating, to generate electricity, and it transported the mills' output away to factories and military depots.

Amid secrecy, Stobs Camp resumed its role for the military making the LNER much occupied with special trains supplying its requirements for food, equipment and munitions. The troops in training were now quartered in Nissan huts and the camp had its own electricity supply. Tank regiments are known to have used its shooting ranges. After the fall of France in 1940, Polish military units came to the Borders, setting up bases at Duns and Kelso, but the Polish 'High Command' was at Peebles. The moors were a training ground for their Armoured Divisions, and occasionally tanks, brought to the Borders by rail, rumbled through the streets of Galashiels. Norwegian soldiers had a company headquarters at Hawick

In contrast to the Depression years, when agriculture was struggling to keep going, farming communities were preparing for unprecedented activity – an extra 1.5 million acres (787,000 ha) were to go under the plough in Britain. As much food as possible was to be produced from

Scotland's 70,000 holdings with the aim of making the nation self sufficient in most requirements. There were ration cards for food to ensure fair shares and adequate nutrition for everyone. The railway hauled the fertilisers and farm machinery to sustain food production, and it distributed the output – grain, potatoes, meat, eggs, milk and other produce. Country goods yards that had languished were busy again. At first, civilian travel had been discouraged, but soon people were urged to go to the countryside to 'Lend a Hand on the Land'. With petrol rationed and many motor vehicles laid up, the railways played a crucial role in passenger transport and numbers actually went up.

Prior to D-Day, the invasion of Europe on 6 June 1944, troop trains and freight vehicles with munitions and equipment flowed south over the Waverley Route in unprecedented volumes, calling for the use of every locomotive that could turn a wheel. The line proved invaluable as a supplementary route to the East and West Coast main lines, and less liable to attack. On Sundays in 1941, the LNER had seven long freight trains running north from Carlisle Canal over the route.

When VE Day came in May 1945, the railway system throughout Britain was completely run down and suffering from prolonged lack of investment. However, unlike continental railways, the British network was sufficiently undamaged to allow a 'make-do-and-mend' solution rather than radical reconstruction. It has been calculated that between 1939 and 1953 the railways suffered a net 'disinvestment', probably equivalent to £15 billion at 2015 prices. It is debatable that the railway system ever properly recovered.

With the 'Big Four' having been managed as one entity, there was now a strong case for continuing to do so. 'Nationalisation', or state ownership of the means of production, was a core policy of the Labour Party, and in July 1945 a Labour government came to power in the first election of the post-war years. So in January 1948, the private railway companies became state-owned as 'British Railways', under the British Transport Commission that also took charge of road transport and canals. This organisation achieved little integration as years of austerity, with the rationing of materials for reconstruction, lay ahead.

Initially there was a big revival in passenger numbers as some restraints of the war years were lifted and people could travel widely again, enjoying a day trip by rail, or possibly a lengthier journey to resorts or holiday camps at the coast. In the Borders, peacetime activities resumed – the Braw Lads Gathering in Galashiels was advertised, as were similar events, first begun in pre-war years at Kelso and Melrose. New 'rideouts' were introduced in the burghs of Jedburgh, Duns and Coldstream to which supporters could come by rail.

British Railways inherited a 'mixed bag' of stock of varying ages – including over 20,000 steam locomotives – but all were given new liveries and insignia. Express passenger engines, after some experimentation, were turned out in Brunswick green, a colour described as 'serviceable', while carriages were red and cream, the so-called 'blood and custard' paint scheme. Under the BTC, the railways were dependent on central government for funding, appointments and strategy. They were expected to pay their way taking one year with another, but overall management was the responsibility of the Rail Executive that set up regional organisations. With a Scottish Region established, 'Caledonian blue' was chosen for its new station signage and 'totems'.

To increase food production, people were urged to 'Lend a Hand on the Land', for example with the potato harvest, and with petrol rationed they had to travel by rail. (Wikimedia)

In 1948 a freak weather event was to bring non-stop running back to the Borders.

On 11-12 August that year disastrous floods deluged the East Coast main line. The summer months had seen exceptionally heavy rainfall, leaving ground saturated. When a moisture-laden wind from the North Sea surged over the East Coast towards the Lammermuir Hills, the lower Tweed basin received a third of its annual rainfall in just five days. More than 4 inches (100mm) of rain fell on very large stretches of upland and the River Tweed rose 17 feet (5m) at Kelso.

With railway staff reporting adverse conditions to Edinburgh Waverley's Control Centre, all rail movements between Scotland and England on East Coast and Border routes were stopped and several branch lines closed. On Thursday 12 August, 'down' trains coming north, including the 10.00am *Flying Scotsman,* were hauled back from Alnmouth and rerouted via Newcastle-Hexham-Carlisle and the Waverley Route – as were other trains from the south. On the East Coast main line, five bridges were swept away with tracks left in suspension.

Reports emphasised the worsening situation – it had become 'impracticable' to shift the down 7.00pm Carlisle to Edinburgh train stranded at Heriot. The following day, an Edinburgh inspector went south with an engine, cautiously traversing the northern portion of the Waverley Route that was littered with debris. He got as far as Borthwick Bank where the 7.02am Edinburgh-Hawick train was successfully rescued and taken back to Waverley Station.

The inspector then went out

In 1948 with nationalisation, British Railways appeared and in 1956 this design was produced for the crest. (Wikimedia)

A train arriving at Galashiels station in the latter 1950s with an A3 locomotive hauling a train of 'blood and custard' coaches. (G Painter)

again, this time to Tynehead where the diverted 10.00am 'Flying Scotsman' from Kings Cross to Waverley from the previous day was trapped by land slips. Food and drink was brought for passengers and arrangements made with the SMT to send buses to free them by road under police escort.

At Galashiels, the main streets were awash, the road bridge at Buckholm Mill was destroyed and Netherdale Haugh was under water. Tenants of houses at Galafoot were evacuated from second storey windows by means of planks stretched across to the railway embankment. Thousands of pounds worth of damage was caused to the mills in the town.

As the northern part of the Waverley Route had suffered landslides between Borthwick Bank and Gorebridge, trains had to go by Haymarket West to access the West Coast main line. Once the Borders lines were cleared, a diversion was in

place – along the Waverley Route as far south as St Boswells, thence by the single line to Kelso. The intact part of the East Coast main line could then be rejoined at Tweedmouth Junction. That summer, the non-stop runs of the Flying Scotsman had just resumed (post 1939) when the floods came. Nevertheless, there was a determination that this prestigious service should continue, with an extra 45 minutes added to allow for speed restrictions – 25mph between St Boswells and Tweedmouth. Using the diversion, the non-stop service resumed on 17 August.

Typically the Gresley A4s were on these runs. At around 460 tons, the expresses were heavy, and having climbed Falahill, there was a stop allowed at Galashiels to take water. However, the top link enginemen at Haymarket depot determined to attempt non-stop running through to Tweedmouth, and then replenish tenders at the water troughs at Lucker before continuing south to London. The first such run was on 24 August, and the first A4 to haul the 'Flying Scotsman' non-stop over the Borders route from Edinburgh to Kings Cross – a distance of 408.65 miles – was No.60028 Walter K Whigham. In total, seventeen such trips were made, nine up and eight down.

These 'non-stops' on the Waverley Route diversion have become a legend, a tribute to enginemen's skills, and to the economies in water and fuel possible with an A4. The only surviving locomotive of that unique 1948 group is Mallard, the world speed record holder for steam traction. Overall, the floods closed the East Coast main line for eleven weeks.

Floods have been a recurring theme in the Borders – originating with summer and winter storms, or from snowmelt – and affecting the railway many times. In September 1927, the Gala's level matched the notorious flood of 1891; in August 1931, there were 'abnormal rains' detaining trains, inundating Bowshank tunnel and causing serious landslides. In 1938 the Jedburgh branch was closed

After the torrential rainstorm of 12-13 August 1948, the down Flying Scotsman hauled by the new A2 4-6-2 Pearl Diver was stranded at Tynehead station by debris.

(Illustrated London News)

by flood and in August 1954, the non-stop 'Elizabethan Express ' was diverted along the Kelso branch owing to flooding on the East Coast main line.

After the 1948 inundations, there were repercussions for Borders branches. With severe damage on the old Berwickshire Railway, Greenlaw to Duns shut completely and St Boswells to Duns closed to passengers. With repairs made, freight returned between St Boswells and Greenlaw. From then on, with passenger numbers shrinking, local services were either reduced or abandoned. If a passenger service closed, inevitably freight would follow at some stage with tracks lifted. In September 1951, the Selkirk branch lost its one passenger train on weekdays.

Although there were proposals for BR's electrification in 1951, the Rail Executive preferred to 'stick with steam', a technology that was well understood, and that relied on UK coal. So new 'Standard' locomotive classes were designed and rolling stock of all steel construction. Nevertheless, a passenger calling at Hawick in the early 1950s, intent on viewing the motive power at shed 64G might see only former North British engines, such as Scotts, Glens, J36s and J37s there. (Sheds at Riccarton and St Boswells were also Hawick responsibilities). Intriguing as this might be, it was not a healthy state of affairs, and the railway was in a state of 'managed decline'. Nevertheless, Hawick continued to be a busy place with locomotives stopping to take water, and expresses being 're-manned' with another crew taking over. The Waverley Route was also a useful diversionary line for West Coast expresses and for the Royal Train on several occasions.

Up to 1955 BR had been 'profitable', covering its capital charges, but its finances then became problematic. With a Conservative government in power, in January 1955 BTC launched its 'Modernisation Plan' to update the ageing rail network and its rolling stock. Major investment over fifteen years was proposed, with a shift from steam to diesel or electric traction. That summer a strike by ASLEF (the union for drivers and footplatemen) damaged BR's market share of passengers and freight further, convincing opinion makers that the railways were 'a lost cause'.

For the Scottish Region, trials of diesel multiple units (DMUs) took place in 1956, the year when 'third class' became 'second'. DMUs on local trains were a sensation as they allowed passengers to travel in much cleaner conditions. In 1958, two car sets from Gloucester Carriage & Wagon displaced steam haulage on several local services from Edinburgh. Launched with the slogan, 'By Diesel Car... is Best by Far', and running between Edinburgh Waverley and Galashiels via Peebles, they took about 1½ hours for the journey. That year there was a break in a railway tradition – the employment of porters ceased. At Borders stations, a welcoming presence disappeared – there was no one to carry cases, lift cycles across tracks or heave luggage on or off guards' vans.

The Border Counties line saw its last regular passenger train in October 1956, thus ending Riccarton's junction status. That railway village in the 'back country', 66 miles (106km) from Edinburgh and 32 miles (51km) from Carlisle, still had no road access. Its primary function was as a civil engineering depot for line maintenance. Sixty residents worked on the railway, many being linesmen – walking the line, tapping in wooden keys, greasing fish plates, weeding the track and trimming edges and banks. Occasionally, there would be rail to re-lay, ballast to spread, or fences to repair. The Waverley Route was meticulously kept.

**Top:** The only surviving locomotive that ran the non-stops over the northern part of the Waverley Route is LNER No.4468 Mallard, now in the care of the National Railway Museum at York. (Dennis Productions)
**Centre:** In the 1950s, Hawick shed continued to be 'home' to former North British locomotives although BR Standard classes did serve on Borders branches. (W S Sellar)
**Bottom:** The former LNER A3 locomotive Bayardo as BR No.60079, is seen with a southbound train at Hawick station's curving platforms on the Teviot viaduct in 1958. (W S Sellar)

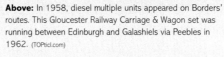

**Above:** In 1958, diesel multiple units appeared on Borders' routes. This Gloucester Railway Carriage & Wagon set was running between Edinburgh and Galashiels via Peebles in 1962. (TOPticl.com)

**Right:** In May 1963, a car transporter train passes Galashiels hauled by a BR Class 4 locomotive, better known as 'Peaks'.
(G Kinghorn)

**Below:** A Metro-Cammell DMU, running between Edinburgh and Hawick, calls at Fountainhall station in November 1968.
(G Kinghorn)

## DIESEL TRAIN SERVICES

EDINBURGH (Waverley) — SUBURBAN STATIONS AND MUSSELBURGH

CORSTORPHINE — NORTH BERWICK

EDINBURGH — PEEBLES — GALASHIELS

From 9th June until 14th September 1958
(or until further notice)

BY DIESEL CAR - - -
- - - IS BEST BY FAR!

**Above:** A handbill for the DMU service tried to entice passengers with the message that such trains were 'best by far'. (Glen Collection)

In 1957, BR revived the name 'Thames-Forth Express' for the day train, but this soon became 'The Waverley'. By 1962 it took 9 hours 17 minutes from Edinburgh to London, compared with 7 hours on 'The Flying Scotsman', but a local advantage was the five stops that it made in the Borders – at Newcastleton, Hawick, St Boswells, Melrose and Galashiels. It was also a useful service in the East Midlands and Yorkshire, but after 1964, 'The Waverley' ran only in summer and ceased altogether four years later.

In 1961 BMC opened its truck and van plant at Bathgate, and for a time the Waverley Route became a long distance freight corridor for its vehicle production going south, while heavy trains of cement, chemical and petroleum tankers also moved north over it. Conveniently, the route straddled the new Millerhill marshalling yard in Midlothian, opened in 1962-3 as part of the Modernisation programme, a site that matched an equally huge yard at Carlisle Kingmoor.

The Transport Act of 1962 established the British Railways Board on which Dr Richard Beeching, a former industrial chemist with ICI, was a board member. Pressure was now on 'to make the railways pay', and in 1963 his report 'The Reshaping of British Railways' identified the profitable businesses for rail as the intercity routes and long distance and bulk freight. The report had been commissioned by Ernest Marples, a Transport Minister with

links to motorway construction. It recommended station closures, the elimination of stopping services and the cutting of secondary routes that duplicated existing lines. This was a threat to the Waverley Route. The 'Beeching Axe' made headlines and there were strong objections from many communities. Even before the cuts took effect, there was another Borders closure – the Peebles line shut in 1962.

The extensive Millerhill yard fronts the modern Monktonhall colliery. A BR Class 26 locomotive is working a train of coal empties on the circuit to Cockenzie power station. (TOPticl.com)

A 'pick-up' freight with B1 BR No.61345 excites attention as it heads south by the Glenfield Road underpass at Galashiels in the 1960s. The young 'train spotters' were with the photographer. (G Kinghorn)

**Right:** After the overwhelming snowfalls of the winter of 1963, BR surfacemen dig out a cutting near Whitrope on the Waverley Route. (W S Sellar)

**Below:** Latterly steam locomotives were hauling long freight trains on the Waverley Route. Here A1 No.60118 *Archibald Sturrock* stands in the lengthy sidings at Hawick in 1963. (W S Sellar)

**Above:** A BR Class 45 passes Heriot station with its level crossing gates while on the up *Waverley* in 1966. (G Kinghorn)

Just when the Beeching Report's dismal news was about to break, winter weather had been most adverse in Scotland with record snowfalls – the worst since 1947. The Waverley Route was hard hit. The first snows in mid-November saw snowploughs running between Hawick and Newcastleton, with serious drifting leaving only a couple of feet under over bridges:

*'The ploughs were usually made up of two engines coupled together, tender to tender with the snow plough in front, but this one had three engines with one pushing in the middle to give extra strength …'* – Riccarton Junction, Recollections of Christopher Millington (1994).

Although the ploughs were continually in use, being supplemented by the Carlisle Canal plough with its two Class 5s, trains became trapped in cuttings 20 feet (6m) deep in snow. Eventually squads were brought from Edinburgh to dig out the drifts near Whitrope. The Waverley Route was blocked for 18 days and had single line working on 25 days that winter.

In the early 1960s, both former LNER and LMS steam locomotives were active on the Waverley Route and enthusiasts especially recall the Gresley A4s, A3s, and V2s with affection. These were however 'cascades', displaced from other services by 'modern traction', were often past their best and principally hauled freight trains. Newer B1s supplemented them, as did former Class 5s and D49s, while Standard Class 4s appeared on local trains.

Prototype diesel locomotives were already in production, some having a poor power-to-weight ratio and others questionable reliability. Many BR diesel classes appeared on Waverley Route trains – from unsuccessful varieties from Clayton Equipment Ltd and the North British Locomotive Company to reputable types from English Electric, BR/Sulzer and Brush. A speculative venture by English Electric in 1955 saw a Deltic, an innovative prototype, take to the rails. Introduced in 1961 as a production series on the East Coast line, Deltics were occasionally observed on the Waverley Route with *Pinza, Crepello* (testing air braking) and *King's Own Yorkshire Light Infantry* being remembered.

In 1964 a Labour government was returned. In the Borders, the railway rundown continued with more service withdrawals – in June, St Boswells-Kelso closed to passengers and in November Galashiels-Selkirk shut for freight. The following year, BR became 'British Rail' with a new corporate identity, a 'double arrow' logo and new uniforms for staff – but these only hid low morale in the industry.

With attempts now being made to save the Waverley Route in its entirety or in part, 'farewell' excursion trains were seen regularly on it. Several were steam hauled – and *Flying Scotsman, Golden Plover, Bittern* and *Blue Peter,* among other notable locomotives, were 'spotted' on the curves at Galashiels. In September 1964, the A4 *Sir Nigel Gresley* made a record breaking run with *'The Scottish Lowlander'* from Carlisle to Edinburgh.

In the 'Swinging Sixties', full employment was reported from Hawick's mills and factories, as there was unprecedented demand for fashion items, with designer labels featuring on knitwear and textiles. Rising incomes were supporting car ownership – possibly as many as one car for every five residents by 1966 – and the unrelenting decline in rail passenger numbers between the Border centres and Edinburgh continued. By now, the trains were seen as inconvenient, dirty and obsolete. There was much

**Top:** School's out and a streamliner's coming! The A4 BR No.60027 *Merlin* looks in good shape as it passes Paterson's siding in Galashiels in the early 1960s. (G Kinghorn)

**Far left:** As car ownership increased, rail services had less relevance; a view in Galashiels in the mid-1950s. (Glen Collection)

**Left:** The British Railways Board had to issue formal notices about the withdrawal of railway passenger services on the Waverley Route, as it did on 17 August 1966. (G Kinghorn)

Newcastleton station looking south – here the Sleeper for London St Pancras was held up by local protesters at the level crossing gates (centre) on 6 January 1969.
(J L Stevenson)

to criticise. The timetable was irregular and five hours might elapse between services, the fare structure was inflexible, and there were few if any attempts to market the line or its trains.

Furthermore, the maintenance of the exposed Waverley Route was expensive, its operation with 26 staffed signal boxes surviving, plus numerous small stations, resulted in the line having the dubious title of the biggest loss maker – reputedly at £500,000 a year – in the Scottish Region. The closure proposal was issued in August 1966 and a protracted debate ensued, as politicians both local and national blew 'hot and cold' over the route's potential, and there was insufficient committed support for its retention. Finance for a takeover was lacking, and eventually BR

management lost patience.

In the Transport Act of 1968, Barbara Castle, the Labour Minister of Transport, had lifted the quantitative restrictions on road haulage that had given the railways protection in 1933. This made competition tougher in the freight sector. Nevertheless, it was recognised that some lines were 'socially necessary but unremunerative' and hence deserving of subsidy. The Waverley Route, a possible contender, fell between two stools – it was neither a rural line in the subsidy category, nor a major 'intercity' link to be developed. After much skirmishing in government circles, the closure was announced by the Minister of Transport Richard Marsh in the House of Commons on 15 July 1968. This was incongruous especially as a plan for economic development in the Central Borders had been drawn up.

In a last ditch effort, John Hibbs, a marketing and transport expert with railway experience, was commissioned by David Steel, Liberal MP for Roxburgh, Selkirk and Peebles, plus local authorities, to investigate transport in the Borders. The Hibbs report was published in December 1968. It advised gearing services to local needs – closing small intermediate stations, issuing tickets on trains and single tracking the line. A case was made for retaining the Edinburgh-Hawick section. What might tourism do for the railway? These were practical suggestions but came too late.

Services continued until 5-6 January 1969 when, amid bitter protests, the last train ran. It was the 21.56 'Sleeper' from Edinburgh Waverley to St Pancras, a popular service with Border MPs and business people returning to London. The protests at Newcastleton made history when local people held the train up at 'their level crossing' for two hours. The parish minister, the Rev. Brydon Maben was

Tracklifting in progress with Class 8 D3889 by the great retaining wall at Ladhope in Galashiels in October 1971.
(G Kinghorn)

Where Hawick station and its tall signal box once stood demolition proceeds in 1975. However the Teviot viaduct is still in place.
(TOPticl.com)

arrested and only freed after the intervention of the MP David Steel who was travelling on the Sleeper.

On the southern part of the Waverley Route, freight ceased between Hawick and Longtown in January 1969 but continued between Millerhill and Hawick until April. Soon tracks were being lifted and stations such as Hawick and Galashiels, with their spacious yards, were 'expunged' from the scene. By 1972, the Scottish Borders was the most extensive and populous area in Britain without a railway. Those Borderers, without access to cars, found buses a slow and uncomfortable substitute on a lengthy and winding road to and from Edinburgh.

For car owners, rail travel had become an irrelevance, just a standby for use in wintry weather – otherwise, most

The textile industry in the Borders experienced serious decline in the 1990s. This aerial view over Galashiels shows the derelict Waverley Mill of 1886 prior to its removal in 2006.
(Hawkeye Scotland)

Railwaymen, many with long service on the Waverley Route, gather for a photo call at the Galashiels signal box in 1970. (G Kinghorn)

took little interest in the railway. The local authorities were at times ambivalent, for example, allowing development on the track bed, and seemingly prioritising road investment. Some Borderers had assumed that those in authority would 'never dare to close the Waverley Route', while others resented the efforts of 'enthusiasts' trying to save the line, in whole or in part.

In 1984 the textile industry, the backbone of Borders manufacturing, was buoyant with an employment peak of 57,000. It had moved from steam power to electricity but the use of new fibres, such as polyester, was a challenge. When intense competition came from overseas producers, rapid decline set in – only 20,000 were left in knitwear and garment making by 2010. This contraction had a detrimental effect on the region as the industry had supported many jobs

An A3 BR No.60052 *Prince Palatine* on a freight is the backdrop for the well kept flower beds and station area at Galashiels in the 1960s. It is the intention that steam locomotives will be seen again on the Borders Railway. (G Kinghorn)

in local economies. With employment opportunities lacking, the Borders became a region with outward migration and the populations of Hawick and Galashiels fell. Some dated these problems to the demise of the railway, but whether a coincidence or a consequence, transport connectivity had been seriously weakened.

There has since been a fight back in the textile sector – it is based on exceptional quality and design with production for niche markets, such as fashion and golf attire. In 1998 Heriot-Watt University's Borders Campus absorbed the School of Textiles and Design at Galashiels. However, better transport links were seen as essential for the Borders long term well doing.

As the years elapsed, reports and studies accumulated. Borders Transport Futures appeared in 1994 and various options were considered – keeping the line open for steam excursions – when BR was intent on banning steam – or developing timber haulage from the Kielder Forest. Tourism was another option. In 1999, it was an incomer, Petra Biberbach whose enthusiasm and contacts with Scottish Enterprise pushed forward the Campaign for the Borders Railway. This brought the Waverley Route to government and public attention again, ensuring that the line's possibilities became a live issue.

In 1999, the Scottish Executive commissioned a feasibility study into the re-opening of the Waverley Route between Edinburgh and Carlisle. Its recommendation was for a line into the Central Borders only. To obtain authorisation to rebuild that railway, 'The Waverley Railway Bill' was lodged in 2003 with the Scottish Parliament, the promoter being Scottish Borders Council. Environmental impact assessments and public consultations began, with representations also being made through MSPs. Enquiries showed that some 94 per cent of local residents were in favour of the line, some hoping for its eventual reinstatement to Hawick.

Meanwhile, in 2002 passenger trains had returned to the northern end of the Waverley Route. The unrelenting expansion of Edinburgh's suburbs led to basic stations being opened at Brunstane, just a single platform, and at Newcraighall, an interchange point for 'park-and-ride'. (These are accessed from Edinburgh Waverley through a 'pinch point' on the East Coast main line at Portobello East Junction, a location in need of re-design, especially with Millerhill yard now designated as a new depot for ScotRail trains).

With a commitment from the Scottish Executive, later the Scottish Government, and with the Bill Committee in place, hearing submissions and entering negotiations began. The outcome was successful and on 24 July 2006, the Act for the Waverley Railway received the Royal Assent. Thereupon, as a symbol of intent and to initiate works on the line, a sod was cut at Galashiels by Stewart Stevenson, Minister for Transport and Infrastructure. The Waverley Rail Partnership, consisting of Scottish Borders Council, Midlothian Council, Edinburgh City Council and Scottish Enterprise, had thus far taken charge of the project, but from then on Transport Scotland, a department of the Scottish Government, would assume that responsibility. After this long gestation period, it now had to find a partner to make the project, renamed the Borders Railway, into a reality.

Footnote: The countdown to the closure of the Waverley Route and its consequences have been examined in depth by David Spaven: see suggested reading.

At Millerhill yad, B1 No.61350 heads south with a train from Edinburgh to Hawick in July 1963. (K M Falconer)

In May 1965, D260 climbs Borthwick bank with an up freight going south on the Waverley Route. (K M Falconer)

In September 1968, D139 ascends Borthwick bank with the up Waverley express from Edinburgh to London St Pancras.
(K M Falconer)

On a summer day in July 1963 B1 No.61350 reaches Falahill with plenty of steam left to make the safety valves lift. (K M Falconer)

Up the 1 in 75 at Borthwick bank comes V2 BR No.60900 working hard on a freight train in September 1961. (K M Falconer)

At a snow covered and deserted Heriot station, D286 hauls a track demolition train on 21 March 1971. (K M Falconer)

It was 'wrong line working' on Borthwick bank on 23 April 1972 for Class 37 No.6919 when the track on the up line had already been lifted. (K M Falconer)

A brief stop at St Boswells for V2 BR No.60955 on the 9.50am Edinburgh Waverley (Saturdays only) train to Sheffield in August 1965.

(K M Falconer)

A B1 pilots a V2 N.61076 on a train of tank wagons at Riccarton Junction in the 1960s. (ColourRail)

In April 1965 V2 BR No.60813, hauling a freight train, tops Falahill with its former inn and railway cottages by the line side.

(ColourRail)

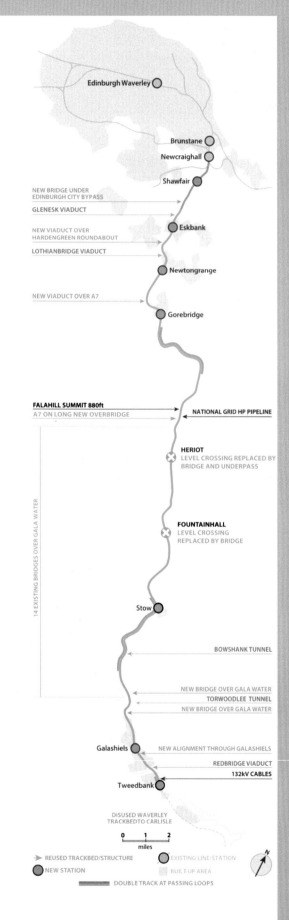

The Borders Railway based on a map from 'Rail Engineer' magazine.

**Top:** The view north at Monktonhall towards Newcraighall and the start of the Borders Railway in October 2012.

**Centre:** Torwoodlee – where nature had reclaimed a former bridge site by the Gala Water.

**Above:** Galashiels – the old track bed beside ASDA in 2012 – there once was a main line here.

# A Waverley Route Revival

ven before a spadeful of earth had been shifted on the old Waverley Route, in 2002 a public relations consultancy had been appointed for the railway project. Soon 'roadshows' in Borders communities were scheduled, and. these were backed by a flood of leaflets and response cards. All the media 'savvy' available to advance the railway's cause and to explain the actions being proposed or taken, was employed using local newspapers, radio and TV – and this 'barrage of information' would be sustained throughout the course of the project. The web site attempted to cover everything relating to the construction – using plans, photographs and video clips. Consultations with community groups were held regularly and there was also ongoing engagement through sports and other public events. Much effort was put into school visits with strong safety messages being given to young people unaccustomed to a railway's proximity.

The cost of the line's reinstatement kept escalating. In 2003 it was £155m, but it soon crept up, and by 2012, it had almost doubled to £294m, pushed by inflation, the complex tendering process, ground remediation, property acquisition and new legislation – for instance, relating to the environment. It now stands at £350m. However, such increases have been typical of major transport projects in Britain, either for railways or for roads.

Unlike the Edinburgh & Hawick Railway where compensation for land and property approached 40 per cent of total costs, the figure for the Borders Railway hovers at 8.4 per cent (based on a target cost for the project of £294m) in 2014. It may take many years until the full costs of compensation are agreed. With over 200 claims entered, 70 were outstanding by 2015; there were some with 'no claims' as yet made, while a few might involve a Lands Tribunal. Among the more unusual items for compensation was a fish farm for rainbow trout at Torwoodlee and another for the tonnes of rock blasted from the historic quarry at Falahill.

In 2008, when Transport Scotland became the mastermind for the Waverley Route's partial revival, the name was changed from the 'Waverley Rail Project' to 'The Borders Railway Project'. Lengthy negotiations ensued with potential consortia for constructing and operating the line – without success. In 2011 it was announced that Network Rail would be Transport Scotland's partner for the construction and delivery of the Borders Railway on the basis of the parliamentary plans. The Network Rail engineering teams, led by Project Director Hugh Wark, had shown their capabilities with the completion of the Airdrie-Bathgate Rail Link in 2010. The documents transferring responsibility from Transport Scotland to Network Rail were signed at the Scottish Mining Museum at Newtongrange on

6 November 2012.

An outline design for the 30½ mile (49km) route had established the principles for its reconstruction. This was taken forward to produce comprehensive drawings of what would be built and how construction would be carried out. As with all aspects of this railway restoration, the maps and plans were available to view on the Internet and in public libraries.

If any residents imagined that the Borders Railway would be only a matter of re-laying track and re-opening stations, they were much mistaken. There were no fewer than 137 bridges – 42 being new or major reconstructions, the remaining 95 in need of refurbishment – all having to be made to comply with current safety standards and permitting the track to run over or under them. Clearances above the line would have to be sufficient to allow for eventual electrification. If any features typify the Borders Railway, it is the multiplicity and variety of its bridges, both old and new

By 2012 some advance works had already begun, including the fencing of sites and the removal of structures built on the track bed. In step with ecological surveys and monitoring, tree felling and vegetation clearance took place out with the nesting season. Amphibian species were also investigated, but no rarities were found. Any works in or near rivers were mindful of salmon spawning months, and when the Gala Water was diverted north of Fountainhall,

Clearing vegetation at Lady Brae near Gorebridge in January 2012.

(M Powers, Network Rail)

**Right:** Putting up bat boxes near Bowshank tunnel. (Network Rail)

**Below:** Scour protection on the Gala Water at Hazelbank. (J Gildea, Network Rail)

store. Before work could begin, the debris on the former tracks had to be scraped away and the old ballast removed. After route closure, as far as structures were concerned, British Rail had retained an obligation to carry out inspections and maintenance on a five-year cycle, or after any emergency such as a bridge strike. This regime continued until privatisation in 1996. The old over bridges still had their BR designations, for example 'OB32' in fading paint, on them.

The surveys out of doors were backed up by desk research. Experts had studied geological maps showing the 'solid geology' of the badly shattered Silurian rocks of 500 million year ago that formed the uplands, and the later Carboniferous formations of the Esk coal basin. The 'drift geology' sheets for the superficial deposits revealed what earth moving machines might encounter – boulder clay, with huge rocks concealed therein, smeared over the land by ice sheets long ago, sands deposited by melt waters, and stretches of peat and alluvium in the river valleys. There was plenty to do before the work on tackling the railway's revival could commence.

With Network Rail in charge and BAM Nuttall appointed as the main contractor, the reconstruction was split into three sections – the North Section ran from Shawfair to Gorebridge, Central from Fushiebridge to Bowshank Tunnel, and South from there through Galashiels to Tweedbank. Overall, the project was managed from the Lady Victoria Industrial Park at Newtongrange. Construction activities stepped up in February 2013. A dry summer plus a mild winter allowed some key milestones to be achieved. At its maximum, there were over 1,000 people at work on the project and 41 access points to sites had been created. Every mile brought a variety of structures for the engineers to confront.

The former northern portion of the Waverley Route crossed the Lothian coal basin. Although records for coalmining extraction from the 1900s were available, there were numerous shallow mine workings some 20-30m deep that predated 1850. Any historic pits beneath the proposed line presented a risk for both the construction and operation of the reinstated railway. To treat the suspect ground, the general principle was to allow 10m of rock cover for every metre thickness of workings. Where there were bridges, stations and other structures, more onerous requirements were applied Accordingly, massive mining remediation was carried out with thousands of boreholes drilled on a grid system down to 20 to 40m on or near the new line. Grout, a liquid mix of ash and cement, was then injected and later, test boreholes were drilled to check the outcome. Where old shafts were identified, 'Bailey bridges' were positioned over these for safe working, and then the cavity was filled with a wedge of grout.

lampreys were removed to temporary locations elsewhere. Once embankment reconstruction was finished, the Gala Water was 'put back' into its present bed. Rare bat species that had lodged in Bowshank tunnel were deterred from returning by sealing crevices, by installing gates at the tunnel mouths and by setting up bat boxes a safe distance away. Avoiding action was also taken with respect to badgers, a protected species.

As the Waverley Route had been out of use since 1969 with rail lifting completed by 1972, the track bed had found other uses – in some places, being 'black path' – tarmac covered cycle ways – and in others, grassy tracks. Over decades, the latter had been compacted by agricultural machinery and the passage of livestock. Bowshank tunnel had been used as a convenient cattle shed and machine

In addition, Monktonhall Colliery, a 'super pit', sunk in 1953, had once stood on an extensive site near Newton in Midlothian. Its coal supplied Cockenzie Power Station by means of merry-go-round trains. Finally closing in 1997, the only evidence for its former existence was its weighbridge, reed beds for the treatment of polluted water, and a landscaped 'bing' or spoil heap. To the east lay the former Millerhill marshalling yard (opened 1961-62) that complimented the immense yard at Kingmoor north of Carlisle, both briefly serving the Waverley Route when it was a freight corridor.

In this area, the new 'town' of Shawfair will be built. This initial development, with 4,000 houses, has been planned

**Left:** Farmers made use of the old track bed for easier access. (Timon Rose)

**Below:** A tarred path on a portion of track bed at Ladhope, Galashiels.

**Right:** Taking soil samples in peaty ground in December 2012.

**Below:** 'Fortress Fountainhall', the main BAM compound for the Central Section, takes shape in May 2013. There were 41 access points to sites on the project. (J Gildea, Network Rail)

**Below right:** Preparing grout for injection into ground once mined for coal at Shawfair in November 2012.

Mining remediation in progress with boreholes being drilled near the Shawfair site in December 2012.

to help alleviate Edinburgh's growing population – a key element in the design of the 'new town' being the railway's revival. Shawfair station, with 'park & ride' facilities, would be the first to be completed on the Borders Railway. (In step with government environmental targets, the most northerly structure on the route is an over bridge giving access to a 'zero waste' facility for Edinburgh).

From Newcraighall the line follows a new alignment compared to the original Edinburgh & Hawick Railway, and

An old mineshaft opened up at Gorebridge station in July 2014.

consequently there was substantial excavation to open out a passage through colliery waste to prepare for the incoming tracks. Over 500,000 tonnes of material was moved, all to be re-used at other sites. Conveniently, Millerhill depot lies to the east, and it was identified as a means of supplying the project with ballast and other services during track laying.

A development on the scale of Shawfair has impacted on the local road system and involved major adjustments to utilities. The railway continues south on its new alignment over farmland towards the A720 Edinburgh city bypass. This sits on an embankment at Sheriffhall and presented a significant obstacle for the project. The solution was to construct a temporary road diversion of dual carriageway some 400m long on the north side. This allowed the building of an over bridge with pre-cast side and deck panels to take the railway beneath the bypass. Meanwhile, the regular flows of road traffic in the area were kept moving as smoothly as possible. The portion of carriageway above the railway was reinstated by May 2014.

From north of Shawfair, there is double track as this is part of the first 'dynamic loop' that extends to Kingsgate on the Dalkeith estate near Eskbank. It is one of three such loops that allow trains to pass at speed. The second is from near Gorebridge to Tynehead, and the third from north of Stow to Bowland. In total, these loops amount to 9 miles (14.4km) of double track – a considerable reduction on the 16 miles (25.6km) first proposed, but passive provision has been made for additional double track at Newtongrange if this should prove necessary.

To form the loops, six sets of prefabricated points with switches and crossings were craned into place in August and September 2014, with an additional set being installed for access to the terminus platform at Tweedbank. Siemens was the sub-contractor for signalling and telecommunications

A 'Bailey bridge' placed over a mineshaft at Fushiebridge in October 2013.

along the railway. By the line side, a small plough first cut a narrow duct for plastic piping through which fibre optic cables could be 'blown'. At each set of points, cabinets receive electricity from the National Grid to operate switches and colour light signals. The telecommunications system has 15 radio masts resulting from the complex and hilly terrain through which the Borders Railway runs. This will allow train drivers to talk to signallers, controllers and management using technology known as GSM-R, a digitally secure method that enhances train safety. The masts serve as 'base stations', and after visual assessment, have been carefully placed to ensure operational effectiveness. On 22 February 2015, another milestone was reached when the Borders Railway was connected into the national signalling system by Network Rail.

South of Sheriffhall the line reverts to the Waverley Route track bed as it goes towards Eskbank and Newtongrange. On the way, the venerable Glenesk viaduct (1831) with its semi-circular arch spans the River North Esk. It now has a pre-cast track trough on top carrying a single line. All such structures on the Borders Railway, whether old or new, have railings and safe access points for maintenance staff. The several over bridges of stone and brick near Eskbank have received masonry repairs, the raising of parapets in the interests of safety, and waterproofing – a routine repeated at other bridge sites along the line. The new Eskbank station

A massive 'plug' of grout caps the mineshaft in July 2014.

**Above left:** In August 2013 the bypass on the A720 was under construction at Sheriffhall.

**Above:** Cutting through boulder clay to prepare for the new 'tunnel', or over bridge, with the road diversion on the A720 now in use.

**Left:** Lifting concrete sections for the 'tunnel' walls in October 2103.

**Below:** The scale of the construction at Sheriffhall becomes clear as the work advances.

**Above:** The bypass at Sheriffhall with the 'tunnel' site in view. (Network Rail)

**Left:** The interior of the new structure to take double track in November 2013.

**Below:** The 'tunnel', soon to be an over bridge carrying the A720, in June 2014 with wing walls nearing completion.

North of Shawfair, a prefabricated crossover was lifted and placed with laser precision in September 2014. Here a double track becomes a single line.
(M Powers, Network Rail)

A similar crossover south of Newcraighall gives access to the national rail system and here a flexible buffer stop was installed.

Laying ducting for fibre optic cables in June 2014. A company in Hawick supplied the fibre optics.

(M Powers, Network Rail)

is located adjacent to the Edinburgh College and several footbridges have been placed over the shallow cuttings in that area

The busy railway yard at Hardengreen has long gone – the site now being occupied by a supermarket – and the road systems here have since had priority. A new viaduct was necessary to take the railway over a roundabout on the A7 Edinburgh-Galashiels road. This modern structure rests on a central pier; with pre-cast concrete beams supporting the deck. Its assembly during road closures was a round-the-clock event. A reinforced earth system, with concrete facing panels, held together with steel reinforcing straps and back filled, has been used for the wing walls. On top, there is a single track with guardrails giving protection against derailment, but the viaduct itself has derailment retention parapets.

Next comes the most impressive feature on the line – the 23-arch Lothianbridge viaduct (1846), variously known as Dalhousie and Newbattle – crossing the valley of the River South Esk. This robust structure permitted the transport of materials 'off road' during construction works. Masonry repairs have included re-pointing and the replacement of defective stone. In the years of the North British Railway, the viaduct's arches and piers were strengthened with bands of bullhead rail and the decision was taken to replace those that were missing, thereby enhancing the appearance of the whole historic structure.

The line soon passes the new Newtongrange station close to the Scottish Mining Museum, located at the former site of the Lady Victoria Colliery. Path access will be made from the station to this visitor attraction. Southwards, the railway continues climbing through parkland where a cutting

The signalling installation completed near Kingsgate in November 2014.

**Above:** The Glenesk viaduct of 1831, spanning the valley of the North Esk, as seen from the air. (Network Rail)

**Left:** Masons at work on new parapets at Glenesk in October 2013.

**Above:** The crucial matter of drainage having attention at Glenesk viaduct.

**Above:** The 'roundabout' gap at Hardengreen, where road improvements had destroyed a railway embankment.

**Below:** Work begins for the new structure at the roundabout site in July 2013.

**Left:** Piling under way at Hardengreen roundabout in October 2013.

**Above:** The piers for the viaduct near completion in January 2014.

**Right:** In February 2014 the concrete beams arrive from Ireland. (M Powers, Network Rail)

**Above:** The scale of the beams dwarfs the engineers on site. (M Powers, Network Rail)

**Left:** The big lift with a 1,200 tonne crane follows. (M Powers, Network Rail)

**Top:** Two cranes in action to place parapets on the new viaduct in March 2014.

**Above:** Fitting RECo panels for the wing walls of the Hardengreen viaduct.

**Right:** Technicians adjust the wire tensioning for the RECo panels.

**Left:** Every effort was made to keep traffic flowing during construction of the Hardengreen viaduct – this is a road user's view.

**Below:** An aerial view of the completed Hardengreen viaduct in November 2014.
(Network Rail)

**Right:** The Lothianbridge viaduct was a useful 'off road' corridor for moving materials.

**Below:** Work in progress on the parapets and drains at Lothianbridge viaduct.

**Bottom left:** Rolling out membrane before bottom ballast is dropped in October 2013.

**Bottom right:** High level repairs on a brick arch at Lothianbridge viaduct in November 2013.

had been filled with spoil from road works. Towards Gore Glen, the line swings eastwards with another remarkable crossing on the A7 – by means of a new under bridge on a slope of 1 in 70 with the track slewed on top. Here interruptions to road traffic were again minimised. After piling and other preparatory work, over a weekend cranes placed pre-cast beams for the bridge on top. The deck was then formed with steel reinforcements and poured concrete. Again, a reinforced earth system for the wing walls has completed this bridge.

The line continues to rise towards Gorebridge – a village once close to the collieries at Arniston and Vogrie – and further treatment of old coal pits was essential here. Considerable slippage along a lengthy cutting had occurred in this area, hence much earthmoving plus stabilising of the slopes was done to prevent any recurrences, and a major drainage system was installed.

Beyond Fushiebridge, the line veers away into countryside past the old granary at Catcune. Here, Borthwick Bank, with its ascent of 1 in 70 begins. This long embankment, with its reverse curves, overlooks the valley of the Gore Water where Borthwick Castle, a fortress dating from 1430, comes into view – hence the name. Both embankments and cuttings have been widened and reinforced – miles of stone- filled drains have been formed and rock blankets used extensively. Along track sides, thousands of gabions – wire baskets packed with stone – now secure the lower slopes on what is another 'dynamic loop' of double track Such measures have also been taken at Tynehead to minimise the risk of landslips and consequent disruption to train services. Accommodation bridges to serve farms have been replaced at Catcune, Halflawkiln and Cowbraehill. Some of these are controversial only permitting clearance for a single track. Surviving over bridges received the standard treatment of repair, strengthening and parapet raising. Shortly, the line crosses from Midlothian into the Scottish Borders.

At Falahill, in a gap between the Lammermuir and

**Left:** Another challenging crossing on the A7 was the new bridge at Goreglen seen with piers for the deck construction in November 2013.

**Below:** The deck of the new under bridge was in place early in 2014.

**Bottom right:** At the new Goreglen bridge, the track has been slewed across the structure and a footbridge has been built further east.
(Network Rail)

**Left:** Filling gabion baskets near Gorebridge station in December 2013.

Tackling drainage in the wet cutting at Gorebridge in August 2014.

Re-shaping the cutting on Borthwick bank in November 2013 with earth moving machines removing boulder clay. (J Gildea, Network Rail)

**Left:** Rock blankets and counter fort protection to improve the stability of slopes at Tynehead in September 2013.
(J Gildea, Network Rail)

**Below:** A big bang when explosives loosened rock at Falahill in October 2013.

Moorfoot Hills, the summit of the Borders Railway is reached at 880ft (271m). There will be an innovation on this part of the Waverley Route – a summit board will be placed here. Although sweeping powers are conferred by an Act for a railway, there are Planning Departments and local authority committees that have also to be convinced if original plans have to be altered. Such an instance arose at Falahill where the intention to have a double roundabout on the A7 was abandoned. A concrete box 'tunnel', some 100m in length, was formed to carry the realigned A7 over the railway. (It is a reversion to past practice at a restricted location where the main road was once on an over bridge above the line). On Falahill itself, rock removed by blasting over many weeks, was stone-crushed and recycled to pack gabion baskets and create rock blankets, while spoil superfluous at other sites was brought to fill the resulting excavations. During the Borders rail project, the aim was self-sufficiency, achieved by the recycling of materials wherever possible. This has saved considerably on transport costs and landfill tax. Elsewhere, soil was reserved to dress banks and allow 'hydro seeding' with grass to begin. The result is that cuttings and embankments quickly lost their raw look.

Moving south to Heriot, in step with Network Rail's policy, an old level crossing has been replaced by an underpass for pedestrians, while for road users an over bridge has been built further south. These have both entailed realignments of roads, extensive construction works around the hamlet of Heriot itself, and the bridging of the Gala Water, (which is just a burn at this point). At Fountainhall, the removal of another level crossing has involved further substantial road works, with a new concrete bridge now positioned over the railway.

The meandering Gala Water is crossed many times on its way to the River Tweed. The restoration of the many malleable iron under bridges, some of them of a characteristic 'hogback' design, has borrowed from 'Forth Bridge' practice, developed when that famous viaduct was refurbished some years ago. So the old bridges were first encapsulated in plastic sheeting (to prevent contamination of the environment)), then grit-blasted and repaired where necessary. The opportunity was taken to re-deck the

At the Falahill site of a former quarry in June 2014, rock excavation was in full swing.

Lorries collected crushed rock for use in filling gabion baskets and for forming stone blankets.

**Left:** The decision was taken to carry the A7 road across the railway at Falahill, necessitating the construction of a long over bridge to take the line. Here scaffolding hides the walls of the concrete 'tunnel' as it takes shape in June 2014.

**Top left:** In August 2014, work in progress on the 'tunnel roof' that will carry the A7 over the line.

**Top right:** A glimpse of the 'tunnel' with the A7 on top in October 2014.

**Opposite top:** A view south over the Falahill site from the air in July 2014 as work proceeds on the long over bridge while road traffic is kept moving on the left. (Network Rail)

**Opposite bottom:** Spoil arriving from other sites by tipper lorry was used to fill the excavation at Falahill where it was spread by bulldozers.

**Left:** The south portal of the 'tunnel' at Falahill approaches completion in October 2014.

**Below:** By March 2014 the re-aligned A7 goes over the railway at Falahill using the long over bridge. (Network Rail)

**Top:** A view of Heriot from the air where an underpass has replaced a level crossing at the former station site. (Network Rail)

**Lower:** South of the village of Heriot, a new bridge on an embankment takes the road over the railway while a large culvert has been contructed for the Gala Water (right).

**Inset:** This image shows the structures at Heriot as seen from the north in June 2014.

structures – though the old timber of pitch pine was in remarkably good condition. In addition, various reinforcement works and repairs to piers and abutments were carried out, the purpose being to fortify the bridges against potential flood damage. Lastly, the metalwork was painted in 'holly green'. Handrails have been fitted and safe access arrangements made for maintenance.

On the single line sections, one side only of a bridge carries track – this may be 'east side' on the old 'Up Line' to London, or 'west side' on the former 'Down Line' to Edinburgh Waverley – the choice being made in order to ease curves. The 'disused' side is then reserved for engineering purposes.

As the railway approaches the village of Stow, the line skirts one of the rocky bluffs along the valley and another dynamic loop begins that extends south to Bowland. At Stow there has long been a community lobby in favour of the Borders Railway, and it is not surprising that this is the only 'rural' station to be reopened on the line. The old station building of 1848 will find a community use. By contrast, the stations in Midlothian are essentially 'suburban', falling within the established commuting zone of Edinburgh.

In the South Section, Bowshank Tunnel 249yd (227.69m) has had special attention. It is approached over the fine lattice girder bridge of 1879 that spans the

**Inset above left:** The malleable iron bridges over the Gala Water were 'encapsulated' in plastic sheeting.

**Above:** With scaffolding in place, the old timber decks were stripped off. (M Powers, Network Rail)

**Below:** After shot blasting, repairs and painting in 'holly green', such bridges looked as good as new. (J Gildea, Network Rail)

The irregular interior of Bowshank tunnel with its
brick lining shows up when the end of a newly
laid rail is cut in January 2014. (Network Rail)

**Above:** Re-working crushed rock and spoil saved outlays on landfill tax and addressed environmental concerns about road haulage over long distances. Here material arrives at Stow station for re-use there. The old station building will find a community purpose. (Timon Rose)

**Below:** In January 2015, a long ballast train approaches Bowshank tunnel from the north, crossing the restored lattice girder bridge of 1879.

temperamental Gala Water. In the tunnel, the exclusion of rare bat species was followed by the checking and repair of the brick lining. The track bed has been carefully lowered to make passive provision for electrification and special slab track, as used in HSL-Zuid (a high speed line in the Netherlands), has been laid. Rails in the tunnel have been treated to resist corrosion.

Immediately south of Bowshank tunnel, there is a new steel and concrete under bridge. A mile further on, the quaint low bridge at Bowland has gone – replaced by a taller version to allow the passage of modern farm machinery – with the embankments on either side having to be raised to accommodate it.

At Torwoodlee estate, an imposing triple-arched masonry bridge straddles a deep cutting. This leads to a difficult section of the line with two major crossings of the Gala Water in quick succession. These bridges were partial replacements, re-using abutments and piers to take new structures – on the north, steel beams were chosen and on the south, concrete. The two bridges are separated by a short tunnel and by a pair of masonry under bridges – making this 'gorge' arguably the most scenic part of the Borders Railway. The line now swings to the southeast towards the former site of Kilnknowe Junction where the branch to Peebles took off from the Waverley Route. The farm bridge at Kilnknowe, built in

**Above:** This aerial view shows Halflawkiln southeast of Gorebridge where a farm bridge had to be replaced. Here a new structure rises beside a temporary access. (Network Rail)

**Top right:** Lifting a steel beam for the reconstructed bridge over the Gala Water in the gorge at Torwoodlee in June 2014.

**Right:** The new under bridge at Ferniehurst with a ballast train crossing in January 2015.

**Centre left:** The over bridge for the new road crossing at Fountainhall takes shape in May 2014.

**Centre right:** Masonry repairs on the old bridge at Kilnknowe that straddled both the Waverley Route (left) and the Peebles branch (right) in August 2013.

**Lower left:** This footbridge near Newton in Midlothian was the last to be completed in May 2015.

**Lower right:** This high level footbridge near Langlee in Galashiels is a contrast in style.

**Above:** A replacement for the low bridge at Bowland takes shape in July 2014. Considerable earthworks were required to raise the embankments for the line here.

**Below:** The 3-arch bridge across the deep cutting at Torwoodlee is on a scenic section of the line with a golf course on the upper levels. (Newtork Rail)

1864 with arches for both double and single track, has been refurbished. The old Peebles line is now a path for cyclists and pedestrians.

Going east towards Galashiels, there has been substantial alteration to the alignment to take the Borders Railway into that town. First, the under bridge at Wheatlands Road was replaced to give a clearance of 5.3m for the passage of fire service vehicles. This heightened bridge has had a 'knock on' effect on adjacent structures – the neighbouring bridge over the Gala Water having to be raised, and the access over the line at Plumtree Brae reconstructed. Overall in this section, adjustments in the levels for the track bed have been essential. For the under bridges in Galashiels, the steel girders have been painted maroon as a gesture to the town's colours for its rugby and football teams.

On the north side of Galashiels, a short tunnel leads to the lengthy brick retaining wall at Ladhope, a dominant feature by the lineside. A new 'shelf' of reinforced concrete panels, faced with sandstone masonry, has been built to carry the track here. This is slotted through what little land is available – the former railway yards now being occupied by a health centre, a supermarket, an industrial estate and housing. There will only be room for a halt with a single platform in Galashiels itself, hence the development of a terminus at Tweedbank. At Ladhope Road, a tall transport interchange building will serve both rail and bus passengers, and have offices above. The railway then goes under Station Brae, part of the town's Inner Relief Road opened in 2007, before curving

The new bridge at Wheatlands Road, with clearance for emergency vehicles, has had an effect on track levels through Galashiels.

**Above:** A view west to Kilnknowe of bridge reconstruction in progress to bring the line into Galashiels in June 2014.
**Left:** Soil nailing on the slope by Station Brae in April 2014.

**Above:** Masons clad the concrete wall supporting the track at Ladhope in central Galashiels with recycled stone in November 2014.

**Right:** The Transport Interchange building rises in Galashiels in May 2014.

**Left:** A massive steel beam for the Currie Road bridge towers over the engineering team at Galashiels in May 2014.
**Below:** It's another heavy lift for the Currie Road bridge at Galashiels.
**Bottom:** The bridge at Currie Road nears completion with masonry and RECo panels in place by February 2015.

From the air, the view over the site at Winston Road by Langlee in East Galashiels also extends to the Red Bridge viaduct across the Tweed. (Network Rail)

**Inset:** Abutments for the new bridge at Winston Road under construction in 2014. (Network Rail)

**Below:** Excavating spoil at the site of the former railway bridge at Winston Road in 2013. (Network Rail)

**Right:** Contructing safe access for track maintenance at the deep cutting at Langlee.

**Bottom:** The bridge site at Winston Road seen from the east in November 2014.

Preparing the track bed with a geotextile 'carpet' prior to bottom ballast being dropped and spread here at Galabank in November 2014. (Timon Rose)

towards Currie Road, where it is carried over on a large new bridge with steel beams. It then passes Glenfield Road on an embankment before entering a long cutting at the foot of the Langlee neighbourhood and the approach to Winston Road.

Winston Road was a strategic site as before a track bed for the Borders Railway could be formed and a new over bridge constructed, a massive landfill deposit had to be cleared. Additionally, utilities embedded therein had to be carefully protected. This work took many months. Thankfully, the Red Bridge, with its five arches over the River Tweed, was intact and here the Borders Railway now shares the crossing with a long distance footpath, the Southern Upland Way. Tweedbank, the railway's terminus, with its island platform and commodious car park, now comes in sight. The intention is that it will be a 'park & ride' hub for other Border towns, serving Melrose, St Boswells, Selkirk and Hawick.

Track laying was eagerly awaited, being a sign of a 'real railway' at last. Once the old ballast was lifted, drainage of the track bed was a priority. With pumps installed to remove standing water, pipes were laid and tanks and culverts formed with sufficient capacity to take rain water or snow melt underneath and away from the line. The foundation for the track was then carefully levelled and a geotextile 'carpet' rolled out preparatory to bottom ballast being dropped and spread. (Ballast is crushed stone that both supports the track and assists drainage).

Through the summer of 2014, some 93,000 concrete sleepers with 'Pandrol' clips to hold the rails were dispersed along the route. A special machine then placed the sleepers at precise intervals where the tracks would

run. The BAM method of track laying, developed in the Netherlands, used an ingenious 'LRU' – a 'long rail unloading' machine – feeding rail lengths of 108m forwards, two at a time down on to the sleepers; this was supplied from a train of wagons propelled by Class 66 locomotives hired from GBFreight. With the rail lengths dropped into position, the clips on the sleepers could then be secured and temporary fish plates fixed at the joints. Subsequently, flash welding joined the cut ends of the rails together.

Placing sleepers on bottom ballast near Shawfair in August 2014.

**Right:** The BAM track laying machines in action near Shawfair in September 2014.

**Below:** Dropping ballast from 'autoballaster' wagons at Kirkhill in October 2014.

Shortly, ballast trains with thirty Network Rail wagons, carrying a total of 1,800 tonnes of stone and topped and tailed by Class 66 locomotives, went gingerly over the newly laid track to spread top ballast – right, left and centre. The red granite ballast was brought to Millerhill depot mainly from Cloburn Quarry near Carstairs. After ballasting came the tamper, usually a Colas-owned machine, to pack the stone firmly under the sleepers. An impressive automatic track finishing machine (AFM) to tidy up the ballast, removing any excess, was also soon

in action. The first section of track was completed at Shawfair on 10 October 2014. A further process involved the stressing of the rail to ensure its stability at a 'stress free temperature of 27°C' – taken as a mean summer temperature in Britain, at which all continuous welded rail in the UK is stressed. The purpose is to reduce the risk of fracturing or buckling of the track when temperature extremes occur.

A crucial principal for the engineers has been to proof the Borders Railway against flood damage. In addition to the devastating floods of 1948, there have been many destructive episodes during the existence of railways in the region. In response to concerns about climate change, the Scottish Executive Central Research Unit carried out a 'Flood Occurrences Review' in 2002 that identified a periodicity in floods at time intervals of 10, 20, 50 and 100 years. It might be fairer to suggest that these events may occur at any time. Efforts have therefore been made to prepare the reconstructed route for potential inundations with a generous provision of drain size and to protect vulnerable places with tipped rock and gabion walls.

There are seven stations on the Borders Railway, namely Shawfair, Eskbank, Newtongrange, Gorebridge, Stow, Galashiels and Tweedbank. All of these are equipped in a similar style to the new stations built on the Airdrie-Bathgate Rail Link, and provide disabled access. They vary in size – whether having one or two platforms, and also according to the car parking provision. The installation of passenger shelters, signage, ticket machines and CCTV followed, along with facilities for cyclists as this aspect of Borders' activities is to be encouraged.

With such a radical rebuilding programme for a railway line over such a length, it was inevitable that there would be

**Left:** Track laying at Newtongrange adjacent to the Scottish Mining Museum and the headquarters for the Borders Railway project in the Lady Victoria Industrial Park, October 2014.

**Below:** The team of track layers and machines advance up Borthwick Bank in October 2014.

Moving ever further south, the track laying train with its Class 66 locomotives is seen at Crookston in gloomy conditions on 14 November 2014. (Peter Delaney)

**Right:** A test of strength? A ballast train with a 1,800 tonne load crosses the viaduct at Hardengreen in October 2014.

(M Powers, Network Rail)

**Below:** Another milestone – track laying reaches the summit of the Borders Railway at Falahill on 6 November 2014.

(J Peter)

**Above:** Blowing snow off sleepers at Ryehaugh near Galashiels on 30 January 2015.

**Left:** Guiding the rails over the sleepers in freezing conditions that day.

**Above:** Two Class 66 locomotives propel the rail carrying train across the reconstructed Ryehaugh bridge.

**Right:** The team head for Galashiels on 30 January with plenty of rail yet to be laid.

**Above:** The track laying team passes the single platform that will serve as Galashiels station on 3 February 2015. (Peter Delaney)

**Left:** Into Tweedbank at last – the rails arrive on 6 February 2015.

(M Powers, Network Rail)

**Right:** Out on the line, and using road-rail machines for access, the welding of rail lengths takes place near Fushiebridge in January 2015.

**Below:** On the west curve approaching Gorebridge station, 'lateral restraint plates' are dropped in March 2015; these are used to stop track moving out of position as temperature varies.

**Below right:** Job done – the lateral restraint plates have been installed between the sleepers on the continuous welded track. A signal post is on the right.

some tribulations. Consultations and public relations' efforts can only take a project so far. The reality of road closures, traffic disruption, mud on roads, wear and tear on surfaces, noise from machinery, flood lighting and so on, tried the patience of some communities as the project advanced.

With driver training on the route commencing on 8 June 2015, the Borders Railway was prepared for its official opening on 6 September – the longest 'domestic' line to be completed in Britain since the 1900s. It is a railway realised by team efforts, with Network Rail leading the project and working with partners to deliver it 'on time and on budget' on behalf of Transport Scotland. It is hoped that many benefits will ensue from this line – encouraging employment, facilitating cultural and social contacts, bringing opportunities for education and promoting tourism. For Borderers, it will be a welcome alternative to the congested and sinuous A7, offering a comfortable journey to Edinburgh of around an hour.

The new line may be viewed as a bonus as it goes beyond Gorebridge. All the Scottish lines that have re-opened have been essentially suburban and aimed at commuters – but the Borders Railway is attempting to be much more than just a commuting route as its purpose is also to be an agent for economic and social

**Above:** A Colas tamper packing ballast under sleepers crosses the new bridge over the A7 at Goreglen in October 2014. (M Powers, Network Rail)

**Below:** An impressive 'AFM' – Automated Finishing Machine – to dress the ballast in action south of Heriot in March 2015.

A view over Shawfair station in March 2015, on land soon to be a hub for the new town in Midlothian. The platforms, footbridge and ramps are in place while the access roads have been completed with car parking in hand. (Network Rail)

Inset above: Advertisement for Shawfair.

Inset right: A Class 158 DMU calls at Shawfair station while on a test run. Such sets will operate most services. (John Peter)

transformation. Towards this outcome, tourism in the Borders is to be promoted – as it was long ago by the North British Railway – and so charter trains will be run. To accommodate these, the platforms at Tweedbank will be sufficient to take 9 coach trains (with tracks long enough for 12 coaches and two locomotives) and this will hopefully give Borders tourism a welcome boost. In addition, Tweedbank is proposed as a heritage centre providing a home for the 'Great Tapestry of Scotland'.

Hitherto, every line reopened in Scotland has either met or surpassed its forecasts for passenger numbers. In the recent decade on ScotRail services, there has been exceptional growth, with the numbers increasing at 3 per cent a year. It is hoped that the Borders Railway will be another success story arising from the revival of this northern part of the Waverley Route.

Some people ask about extending the line to Hawick, notwithstanding the difficulties of negotiating a route through Melrose and St Boswells. Furthermore, there are enthusiasts who toy with the idea of a new Waverley Route all the way to Carlisle, this time going via Langholm. They are encouraged by the thought that railway revivals that were initially looking most unlikely are taking place in Britain.

**Opposite:** Shawfair station at an earlier phase with a crane lifting the access ramps in November 2014.

**Below:** Stow station with a Class 158 DMU on the 'down line' on 8 June 2015 prior to driver training commencing. (Peter Delaney)

A Network Rail test train at Galashiels passes the town's halt adjacent to the Transport Interchange (seen on the left) on 8 May 2015.

(Peter Delaney)

A Class158 DMU leaves Tweedbank, the terminus of the Borders Railway on 8 June 2015. Here extensive car parking will attract people from other Border towns to travel by rail.

(Peter Delaney)

# Acknowledgements

It is a source of pride that Lord Steel of Aikwood, who has such a long association with the Borders and its railways, kindly agreed to write the foreword for this book.

Many people and organisations have given assistance and special thanks go to the Scottish Association for Public Transport that has also argued for the re-opening of part of the Waverley Route, now the Borders Railway. First Group and Abellio have supported travel for research purposes.

The author is greatly indebted to Hugh Wark, Project Director for the Borders Railway, for his guidance when preparing progress reports for 'Modern Railways', and for reviewing the chapter on construction. Special thanks are due to Martin (Paddy) Powers, Assistant Construction Manager, Network Rail, for sharing his railway knowledge plus interest in photography, while viewing work in progress. James Gildea, Construction Manager, Network Rail, both explained construction techniques and made images available for this book. Thanks also go to Nissar Mohammed, Project Director, BAM Nuttall.

In reading the typescript and commenting thereon, the contributions of Andrew Boyd and John Yellowlees have been invaluable. Bruce Peter also advised on points of information and style.

Ken Falconer has generously allowed his colour slides to be used while Stuart Sellar has similarly made his unique photographs available. In addition, Hamish Stevenson has loaned his extensive collection while Bill Lynn has contributed station images. The inclusion of aerial views, taken by Tony Gorzkowski of Whitehouse Studios, was permitted by Network Rail. Douglas Squance is thanked for making the George Kinghorn photographs from the 1960s known.

Timon Rose arranged 'forays' into the Borders and allowed the use of his photographs, as have Peter Delaney and Gerry Rudman. Other images have come from ColourRail, from Edward Z Smith, from David Hey and from Derek Robertson. Support from Ilecsys, suppliers to the rail industry, made additional images possible.

The North British Railway Study Group members, led by Donald M Cattanach, have answered questions, while Euan Cameron has contributed his fine drawings of locomotives. The assistance of Paul Wilkinson, Office of Rail Regulation (ORR) and of Simon Gough, Parliamentary Archives in the House of Lords Library, has been most welcome. The Duke of Buccleuch and Queensberry, through the work of Professor David Munro, has permitted the use of plans from the Buccleuch Archives.

Among others who have helped are Bob Hogg, Construction Manager, Network Rail, Sarah Duignan, Network Rail, Bob Burgess of The Southern Reporter, Ronald Morrison of the Borders Family History Society, Ken Bogle, Geoff Corner, Brian Farish, Barrie Forrest, Bruce Gittings, Andrew Murray, Zilla Oddy, Roland Paxton, Elizabeth Pryde, David Shirres, and Jeremy Suter.

The Royal Archives at Windsor Castle, have allowed excerpts from Queen Victoria's Journal to be reproduced with the gracious permission of Her Majesty Queen Elizabeth. Staff at the Department for Transport, the National Archives of Scotland and the National Library of Scotland, especially the Map Library, are also thanked for allowing the reproduction of images. Assistance has also been obtained from the following:

Airdrie Public Library, Edinburgh Public Library, Hawick Callants Club, James Pringle of Torwoodlee, Melrose Rugby Football Club, Midlothian Public Library, Science & Society Picture Library, The Heritage Hub in Hawick, The Mitchell Library and the Royal Commission on Ancient and Historic Monuments of Scotland.

Ian Allan Ltd and Rail Engineer magazine have allowed maps of the Borders rail network to be reproduced; the latter were originally drawn by G. Bickerdike and have been revised by Richard Kirkman.

John Peter offered transport to the Borders on many occasions and prepared the images for this book. Photographs without credits have been taken by the author and are her copyright.

Every effort has been made to trace copyright holders of images and apologies are offered to any who have been overlooked or found untraceable.

'The North British Railway' in two volumes (1975) and

Martin 'Paddy' Powers on the restored Lothianbridge viaduct with a Class 66 locomotive No.736 *Wolverhampton Wanderers* from GB Railfreight.
(Network Rail)

# Suggested reading

'Scotland, Vol. 6, The Lowlands and the Borders' in a 'Regional History of the Railways of Great Britain' (revised by Alan J S Paterson, 1984), by John Thomas, and published by David & Charles, have stood the test of time.

Some other books recount aspects of the Waverley Route:

Main Lines Across the Border, O.S Nock and Derek Cross (Ian Allan Ltd. 1982)

Scottish Region: A History 1948-1973, A.J Mullay (Tempus 2006)

Last Years of the Waverley Route, David Cross (Oxford Publishing Company 2010)

Waverley Route, the battle for the Borders Railway, David Spaven (Argyll Publishing 2015)

For station history along the Waverley Route, there is a series 'Carlisle to Hawick' (2010), 'Hawick to Galashiels' (2013) and 'Galashiels to Edinburgh', (2013) all by Roger Darsley and Dennis Lovett (Middleton Press).

The train advertising the Borders Railway and the attractions in the regions through which it runs – a Class 170 DMU in disguise at Waverley station in April 2015.